Do You Want to
BE HEALED?

"*Do You Want to Be Healed?* is a powerful resource that leads us through scriptural characters, so like us, to discover God's nearness and his desire to heal us."

Mother Gloria Therese, OCD
Superior General
The Carmelite Sisters of the Most Sacred Heart of Los Angeles

"*Do You Want To Be Healed?* is like having a personalized retreat with Bob Schuchts. Having done many retreats with Schuchts, I know that is a special gift. As he guides you through this book, he doesn't want you to encounter himself, he desires for you to encounter the healing love of Jesus. That was my experience of this book and that is what makes it very special."

Jake Khym
Executive director of Life Restoration Ministries
Cohost of *Restore the Glory* podcast

"This ten-day retreat will restore your dignity as a child of God and I highly recommend it to anyone looking to grow as a disciple."

Regina Boyd
Licensed therapist and founder of Boyd Counseling Services

"Having personally experienced the anointed ministry of Bob Schuchts and his team at the John Paul II Healing Center, I am confident that this retreat experience has the potential to change lives forever."

Archbishop Alexander Sample
Archdiocese of Portland

"Do You Want to Be Healed? gently but firmly dares you to meet Jesus's gaze and to risk allowing him to search more deeply and probe afresh the unspoken yearnings of your heart. Experience this scriptural retreat because when Jesus brings the word of his power to bear on your honest yearnings, what happens to them is so profound that you will never be the same."

Sonja Corbitt
Author of *Unleashed*

"This book is a welcome and reliable guide to helping ordinary Christians come to know the healing love of Jesus in areas of physical, emotional, and spiritual pain."

Fr. Mathias Thelen
President of Encounter Ministries

Do You Want to
BE HEALED?

A 10-Day Scriptural Retreat with Jesus

BOB SCHUCHTS

Foreword by Fr. John Burns

AVE MARIA PRESS   AVE   Notre Dame, Indiana

Nihil Obstat:	Very Rev. Canon Héctor R.G. Pérez y Robles, S.T.D., C.S.L.J. Censor Librorum
Imprimatur:	+William A. Wack, C.S.C.
	Bishop of Pensacola–Tallahassee
	Given at Pensacola, FL on 6 April 2022

The *Nihil Obstat* and *Imprimatur* are official declarations that a book or pamphlet is free of doctrinal or moral error. No implication is contained therein that those who have granted the *Nihil Obstat* or *Imprimatur* agree with its contents, opinions, or statements expressed.

The content for the meditations for each day is excerpted from *Be Healed* by Bob Schuchts (Ave Maria Press, 2014).

Founded in 1865, Ave Maria Press is a ministry of the United States Province of Holy Cross.

www.avemariapress.com

Paperback: ISBN-13 978-1-64680-158-9

E-book: ISBN-13 978-1-64680-159-6

Cover image © Thinkstock.com and Unsplash.com.

Cover and text design by Andy Wagoner.

Printed and bound in the United States of America.

Library of Congress Cataloging-in-Publication Data is available.

CONTENTS

FOREWORD BY FR. JOHN BURNS   ix

INTRODUCTION   xvii

DAY 1: "WHO WILL SATISFY   1
YOUR THIRST?"
Awakening Holy Desire: Jesus and the
Samaritan Woman (John 4:7–29)

DAY 2: "DO YOU WANT TO BE WELL?"   13
Rekindling Our Hope: Jesus and the Man
at the Pool of Bethesda (John 5:1–15)

DAY 3: "WHY DO YOU CALL ME GOOD?"   25
Prioritizing Pure Love: Jesus and
the Rich Official (Luke 18:18–30)

DAY 4: "DO YOU BELIEVE THAT   37
I CAN DO THIS?"
Restoring Our Faith: Jesus and the
Two Blind Men (Matthew 9:27–31, 35–38)

DAY 5: "DO YOU KNOW THE   49
FATHER'S LOVE?"
Reclaiming Our Inheritance: Jesus Tells
the Parable of Two Sons (Luke 15:11–32)

DAY 6: "WHAT ARE YOU THINKING   63
    IN YOUR HEART?"
    Healing from the Inside Out: Jesus and
    the Paralyzed Man (Luke 5:17–26)

DAY 7: "HAS NO ONE CONDEMNED YOU?"   75
    Embracing God's Mercy: Jesus and the
    Adulterous Woman (John 8:2–12)

DAY 8: "CAN YOU DRINK THE CUP?"   87
    Redeeming Our Suffering: Jesus and
    His Disciples (Part 1) (Mark 10:35–45)

DAY 9: "HAVE YOU COME TO BELIEVE?"   99
    Unleashing the Sacraments: Jesus and
    His Disciples (Part 2) (John 20:19–29)

DAY 10: "DO YOU LOVE ME MORE   111
    THAN THESE?"
    Resurrecting Our Mission: Jesus and
    Peter (John 21:1, 7, 9, 12–17)

CONCLUSION   123

NOTES   127

FOREWORD
BY FR. JOHN BURNS

In opening this book, you have set your foot on a very sacred path. It is the path that leads you, wherever you find yourself in this present moment, to engage the passageways of your own story. But unlike any other method of engagement, here you will learn to revisit your whole story in a new light, the only true and perfect light—that of Jesus Christ. The journey that you are about to begin will secure your story in the grandest and most magnificent story of all: the story of a Love that saves.

It is a fact of our fallen existence that we all carry stories marked by sorrow, pain, and trial. In our suffering, we so easily succumb to the whispers of a creeping and unholy anxiety. We conclude that our brokenness makes our lives repulsive and worthy only of rejection. Under the weight of these whispers, we learn to live with darkness and keep our broken places hidden. The survival pattern of hiding in loneliness is an ancient one; it comes to us from our first parents, who hid from God and from one another beneath the weight of shame.

When sin entered the hearts of man and woman, Love was interrupted. The rupture tore a hole in the human heart that would ache unto eternity. Yet in infinite kindness, the Lord never tires of asking us the same question he asked the first man and woman when they discovered their nakedness and fled from him: "Where are you?"

Whenever I read that passage from Genesis 3:9, I am always pierced by what I believe is God's tone; it is the tone of a Father who aches for one who has left him and now suffers so. Thenceforth, God would speak through the prophets, over and over, to lovingly interrupt the interruption and restore all things: "Return to me with all your heart" (Jl 2:12).

Wonderfully, God speaks that invitation to you as you read these very words. Ponder that for a moment. What does it stir within? Often, the idea of coming back to God is both attractive and daunting. As desirable as it is, a real and vulnerable return to God seems to come at such a cost. What if those fears are true—what if, when you are truly seen, you will be rejected, found unworthy, condemned for your failings, cast aside as too broken?

Please hear me here: those fears are empty. What you will discover instead is the persistent and searching heart of a God who pours out an unrelenting love that is unlike anything else you will ever know. With each engagement of the broken places within, you will hear Jesus speak tenderly against those fears: "I will not reject anyone who comes to me" (Jn 6:37).

Sometimes we need the help of a friend to begin. Perhaps the disciples' words to the blind man may be of service to you here: "Take heart; rise, he is calling you" (Mk 10:49). Like the disciples, the kind mastery of Dr. Bob Schuchts will come to your aid throughout this book. Dr. Schuchts will invite you to explore passages of your own heart that may well have been abandoned, closed off, or left for dead. He will do so with a very particular focus as he accompanies you in a work that is as vital as any other in your life: the prayerful engagement of sacred scripture as it comes to bear upon your broken heart.

A few thoughts on scripture and story may help frame the significance of this work. In her wisdom, the Church reminds us that the words of sacred scripture were recorded by human writers under the inspiration of the Holy Spirit. The texts of scripture are thus unlike any other written or recorded text; rather than static words on a parched page, the words of the Bible are *alive*. On the "other side" of every passage of scripture is the Spirit of the living God.

The traditional practice of lectio divina brings scripture to life in the soul of the believer. In a wondrous fashion, as we engage the texts of scripture over and over throughout our lives, we discover that God is never finished speaking, guiding, and revealing his solicitude for us. His is a fierce and unrelenting love, a searching force that is at once fearless and tender as it comes to rescue the beloved from every snare.

In human love, every lover who ever whispered that tender phrase, "I love you," has borne a piercing truth: Spoken word can only dimly capture the heart's posture toward the precious other. Because love is a living and transcendent force, its expression grows, develops, and deepens throughout life. For this reason, the lover and the beloved never tire of expressing their love to one another; no true lover ever spoke those words once and considered it enough. Yet human love, as beautiful as it is, offers us but an imperfect prelude, a veiled glance into God's love. "I have loved you with an everlasting love" (Jer 31:3). Indeed, faith draws us into a love that never ends.

Sacred scripture most fittingly quickens the flames of love that flicker and expand in the heart of the beloved. Over and over, year after year, we return to the same familiar passages and find fresh and novel insight. We are never finished contemplating the mysteries contained in scripture because God is never finished speaking to his beloved.

In a captivating and sometimes underemphasized parallel, our stories have more in common with scripture than we might realize. There is only one Spirit of God, and the Spirit who dwells beneath every word of scripture is the same Spirit who holds us in being. We live and move and breathe because God has placed his Spirit within us. As long as we are alive, we are upheld by the constant choice of God, the choice that we should be rather than not be.

As the texts of scripture offer an endless opportunity to encounter the real and true story of God's love for his people, our lives are actually marked by the same character. While scripture contains the universal truths necessary for salvation, our own stories are, in an analogous and personal sense, marked by God's animating presence and providential guidance toward salvation.

As God inspires us to glean new insights from the texts of scripture, so too does God inspire us to recognize new insights about the pathways of our lives that have brought us to this present moment. Our stories, in fact, are filled with epiphanies of love.

What, then, are we to make of the very real state of our hearts, especially while there are those places that still feel filled with bitter pain? We often ask how a good God could have allowed the dark moments and great trials that seem to define our limits. St. Augustine reminds us of the power of God here: "God is so good that in his hand, even evil brings about good. He would never have permitted evil to occur if he had not, thanks to his perfect goodness, been able to use it." The gift of healing unfolds as the Lord comes to us to show that our stories fit into his. As God revisits the story with us, we discover that every wound bears a potency to become a manifestation of Christ's victory over sin and death.

Into any place that you feel the darkness cannot be overcome, I offer a few simple words: In the pages and the prayer that await you here, you will find a pathway through. You will learn to breathe again with God, and to breathe deeply. You will discover that your story is actually magnificent and unrepeatable, that God chooses you *with your whole story*. You will find that nothing is lost, nothing is inconsequential, and the only thing in your journey that is repulsive to God is the sin that He has come to lift from you. The rest—all of the rest, your entire life—is a delight to the Lord. You will be *pierced* by the power of the truth: "The light shines in the darkness, and the darkness has not overcome it" (Jn 1:5).

The path before you will reveal something profoundly true, if you have eyes to see: Your story and your life are of intense interest to God, *who wishes to make you well*. The Lord wants to come into all of the scattered and hidden places to draw everything back together, to bind it up, and liberate you from captivity.

This, friends, is the power of Love, of God who awaits your permission. In such tender strength, Christ beholds you in this very moment, as you are about to begin. And in all his omnipotent kindness, he asks: "Do you want to be healed?"

INTRODUCTION

Do you want to be healed? This was the provocative question Jesus asked the lame man near the pool of Bethesda. It is also the probing question he puts before each one of us as we seek healing in our own lives. We may be hesitant for a myriad of reasons, but Jesus is not deterred. He approaches us fully confident in the Father's love and healing power. The gospels are filled with astonishing stories that demonstrate this reality.

These stories describe Jesus's interactions with people like you and me who have suffered from various physical, psychological, and spiritual afflictions. In these descriptions, we see the weakness of our fallen human condition and our desperate need for healing. We also observe Jesus's kindness and tender compassion for each person he encounters. He heals each person who approaches him with humility and faith.

Over many years of praying with these gospel stories, I am convinced that they are windows into Jesus's heart and mission. Jesus came to save us, and his healings are a demonstration that "God has visited his people" (Lk 7:16). In applying these gospels today, I have come to believe that Jesus is just as eager to heal each one of us as he did the people he encountered two thousand years ago in the Holy Land. I have personally experienced this reality in my own life and have witnessed it repeatedly within my family and in the lives of many others. Many of these experiences are described in my first book, *Be Healed* (Ave Maria Press, 2014).

The book you now hold in your hands is designed as a personal retreat to lead you into your own healing encounters with Jesus. It is organized around ten compelling gospel stories which inspired *Be Healed*. These gospel passages are presented here so that you can pray and reflect on them for your own personal healing.

Throughout this retreat, you will be guided in praying with these ten gospel narratives through a process called lectio divina (which means "divine reading"). This method of encountering Jesus through the gospels has been practiced by the faithful for millennia. Pope Benedict XVI speaks of its potential in his written exhortation *Verbum Domini (The Word of God in the Life and Mission of the Church)*: "*Lectio Divina* . . . is truly 'capable of opening up to the faithful the treasures of God's word, but also of bringing about an encounter with Christ, the living word of God'"(87). This is the goal of this scriptural retreat: to encounter Jesus Christ in the specific areas where you personally need and desire healing.

HOW TO USE THIS RETREAT

This retreat is arranged into ten separate "days," each one dedicated to praying with one of the ten selected gospel passages. It is designed intentionally to adapt to your life circumstances. These "days" can be entered into over a span of ten hours, ten days, ten weeks, or however works best for you. Furthermore, you may engage in these "days" on your own, with the guidance of a spiritual director, or with your family or community. As you prepare for each time of prayer and reflection, try to find a space that will allow you quiet, without distraction. This could be in your home, at a retreat center, at church in front of the Blessed Sacrament, or outside in your favorite place in nature. I encourage you to come to these prayer times with a journal or tablet, so you can record your prayer experiences and deepen the graces over time.

In whatever way you choose to enter into this retreat, give yourself ample time to engage each day with an open mind and receptive heart. Don't rush through these prayer times. Feel free to stay on any one day for as long as you desire, or come back to it repeatedly over time, trusting that Jesus desires to heal and sanctify you, body, soul, and spirit (see 1 Thessalonians 5:23).

While praying with the selected gospel passage for each day, you may also want to read the corresponding section of *Be Healed,* which will add understanding and encourage your faith in Jesus's desire to heal you. However, it is not necessary for you to read *Be Healed* to benefit from this retreat. You can freely engage in this retreat even if you have not read *Be Healed.* As you approach each day, simply walk through the process as it is laid out in this book. Most importantly, allow the Holy Spirit to guide and inspire you as you prepare for "an encounter with Christ, the living word of God" (*Verbum Domini*, 87).

Preparation

Each day opens with the following guides to prepare you mentally, emotionally, and spiritually:

Thematic Question: The theme for each day centers around a specific question posed by Jesus. These questions are drawn, directly or indirectly, from the gospel stories themselves. Approach these questions with the understanding that they are directed to you personally. They are meant to provide a focal point for your reflection.

Invoking God's Presence: As you begin each time of prayer, acknowledge God's presence. Then intentionally invite the Holy Spirit to guide you. The Holy Spirit will bring the gospel passage to life in the here-and-now and lead you into a personal healing encounter with Jesus.

Preview of the Gospel Passage: Before praying with the gospel passage reflect on the insights from the *Catechism of the Catholic Church* (*CCC*) or from St. John Paul II. These quotes are intended to help you focus your attention as you pray through the gospel while employing the lectio divina method.

Lectio Divina

Lectio divina's five basic movements make up the core of each day's reflection. These are reading, meditation, vocal prayer, contemplation, and action. Move slowly and deliberately through each step in the process:

Gospel Reading (***Lectio***): The gospel passage for each day describes an encounter between Jesus and a person in need of healing. Read the passage slowly and prayerfully, with a desire to know how Jesus responds uniquely to each person in their need. Each day's gospel selection corresponds to parallel sections of *Be Healed*. The first five gospel stories are drawn directly from those referenced in the introduction and first four chapters of *Be Healed*. The last five gospel passages are closely associated with the remaining chapters of *Be Healed*.

Meditation (Meditatio): The meditations are drawn from the corresponding chapters of *Be Healed*. They are meant to stir your personal reflections and to awaken your desire for healing. After prayerfully reading the gospel, pause to apply it personally. The Church teaches: "To meditate on what we read helps to make it our own by confronting it with ourselves. Here, another book is opened: the book of life. We pass from thoughts to reality" (*CCC*, 2706).

Vocal Prayer (Oratio): "Following this comes prayer *(oratio)*, which asks the question: what do we say to the Lord in response to his word? Prayer, as petition, intercession, thanksgiving and praise, is the primary way by which the word transforms us" (*Verbum Domini*, 87). Each day, this section on vocal prayer begins with a few verses from one of the psalms and continues with your personal conversation with Jesus or the Father. It may be helpful in this prayer to imagine yourself in the gospel scene, so that you are seeing Jesus (in your sanctified imagination) in front of you and speaking directly to him.

Contemplation (Contemplatio): Contemplation allows you to engage the gospel passage with both your mind and your heart. Placing yourself in the gospel story, identify with the afflictions, doubts, and faith of the person encountering Jesus. Then bring those to Jesus to receive his powerful healing love.

Action (Actio): The people who encounter Jesus in each of the gospel stories respond with a definitive action that demonstrates their faith and actualizes their healing encounter. At the end of each contemplative prayer experience, you are presented with a suggested action, or an opportunity to choose an alternative action, to actualize your healing encounter.

Wisdom from the Church

As Jesus heals us personally, he brings us into deeper communion with his mystical body, the Church. In this section, you will have the opportunity to ground your experience in the Church's wisdom, which is essentially the wisdom of the Holy Spirit speaking to us in our current life circumstances. Each entry will highlight a different aspect of the gospel passage and reflections.

Further Growth

Finally, each day closes with suggestions for further growth, including books to read, videos or movies to watch, and songs to listen to. These suggested resources are intended to provide a deeper understanding of the gospel theme so that you can integrate and expand your healing encounter more fully into your daily life. As you move through this retreat experience, I pray that Jesus's healing love may strengthen and sanctify you in body, soul, and spirit.

"WHO WILL SATISFY YOUR THIRST?"

Awakening Holy Desire: Jesus and the Samaritan Woman

John 4:7–29
(Based on the Introduction to *Be Healed*)

PREPARATION

Place yourself in the presence of God.

The gospel account describing Jesus's encounter with the Samaritan Woman (at Jacob's Well) invites you to examine how you have attempted to satisfy your spiritual thirst in ways that have ultimately left you unfulfilled. We see in this story that only Jesus will satisfy our deepest desires. The *Catechism of the Catholic Church* affirms this reality: "The desire for God is written in the human heart, because man is created by God and for God, and God never ceases to draw man to himself. Only in God will he find the truth and happiness he never stops searching for" (*CCC*, 27).

LECTIO DIVINA
Gospel of John (4:7–29): Jesus
Encounters the Samaritan Woman

Take a few deep breaths. As you breathe, invite the Holy Spirit to inspire you as you pray with this scripture passage.

Reading

As you read through the story slowly, pay attention to how Jesus initiates the conversation with this woman. Notice how he first meets her at a human level and then reveals her troubled relational history before offering her the fulfillment she deeply desires. Finally, notice how the woman responds to Jesus and then goes to tell others about him after this encounter.

[7] A woman of Samaria came to draw water. Jesus said to her, "Give me a drink." [8] His disciples had gone into the town to buy food. [9] The Samaritan woman said to him, "How can you, a Jew, ask me, a Samaritan woman, for a drink?" (For Jews use nothing in common

with Samaritans.) [10] Jesus answered and said to her, "If you knew the gift of God and who is saying to you, 'Give me a drink,' you would have asked him and he would have given you living water." [11] [The woman] said to him, "Sir, you do not even have a bucket and the well is deep; where then can you get this living water? [12] Are you greater than our father Jacob, who gave us this well and drank from it himself with his children and his flocks?" [13] Jesus answered and said to her, "Everyone who drinks this water will be thirsty again; [14] but whoever drinks the water I shall give will never thirst; the water I shall give will become in him a spring of water welling up to eternal life." [15] The woman said to him, "Sir, give me this water, so that I may not be thirsty or have to keep coming here to draw water."

[16] Jesus said to her, "Go call your husband and come back." [17] The woman answered and said to him, "I do not have a husband." Jesus answered her, "You are right in saying, 'I do not have a husband.' [18] For you have had five husbands, and the one you have now is not your husband. What you have said is true." [19] The woman said to him, "Sir, I can see that you are a prophet. [20] Our ancestors worshiped on this mountain; but you people say that the place to worship is in

Jerusalem." ²¹ Jesus said to her, "Believe me, woman, the hour is coming when you will worship the Father neither on this mountain nor in Jerusalem. ²² You people worship what you do not understand; we worship what we understand, because salvation is from the Jews. ²³ But the hour is coming, and is now here, when true worshipers will worship the Father in Spirit and truth; and indeed the Father seeks such people to worship him. ²⁴ God is Spirit, and those who worship him must worship in Spirit and truth." ²⁵ The woman said to him, "I know that the Messiah is coming, the one called the Anointed; when he comes, he will tell us everything." ²⁶ Jesus said to her, "I am he, the one who is speaking with you."

²⁷ At that moment his disciples returned, and were amazed that he was talking with a woman, but still no one said, "What are you looking for?" or "Why are you talking with her?" ²⁸ The woman left her water jar and went into the town and said to the people, ²⁹ "Come see a man who told me everything I have done. Could he possibly be the Messiah?"

Meditation

"This encounter with him, as it burns us, transforms us and frees us . . . enabling us to become truly ourselves and thus totally of God," Pope Benedict XVI writes in his encyclical *Spe Salvi (Saved by Hope).*

Somewhere deep inside each one of us is a burning desire to finally become the person God created us to be. Yearning to be fully alive, we long to give ourselves wholeheartedly back to God. Yet despite these stirrings, many of us hesitate and resist, fearing the very thing we desire. While we long to be made pure and whole, we avoid God's process of purification and healing. I wonder if the Samaritan woman felt a similar reluctance before encountering Jesus at Jacob's well (see John 4). Do you remember her story? Her brief but powerful encounter with Jesus exposed the secrets of her heart and set her free to love again. She came to the well with an insatiable *thirst.* Her many worldly lovers had left these cravings for love unfulfilled. Neither could she satisfy their consuming appetites. One by one, they had thrown her away like a day-old beverage that had lost its taste. We can only imagine how hopeless and unworthy she felt before her encounter with Jesus. Consider her shock when Jesus approached her, asking her for water.

According to the customs of the time, a Samaritan woman would not be permitted to speak with a Jewish man. Furthermore, some scholars suggest she came late in the day to avoid facing the people in her own village. But Jesus was not a bit surprised by their encounter. Coming to the well, Jesus too was *thirsty*, though he was seeking more than water. He thirsted for this woman, with a deep desire that was totally different from the way the other men desired her. While they sought to consume her for their own pleasure, Jesus longed to satisfy her thirst by pouring himself out on her behalf. He desired to fulfill her, not to use her.

Can you picture the scene as they greet each other and his gentle gaze meets hers? I envision her immediately avoiding eye contact with Jesus. But then sensing something unusual in his presence, I imagine her looking up, being drawn into Jesus's penetrating gaze. Piercing her shame and reaching to the depths of her soul with his words, he sees her and speaks to her heart as no one has done before now. His searing love purifies her heart, burning away the shame-based lies that have tarnished her self-respect. Her previously unreachable well, the well of her soul, is now overflowing with living water. Running into the village, she longs to offer a refreshing drink to everyone she meets. She is radically transformed by her encounter with Jesus. Seeing her own dignity for the first time, she now desires to give herself completely to God. She wants to tell everyone about this man who "knew everything" about her. She invites all of us to come and meet him for ourselves.

Vocal Prayer

Express your desires directly to Jesus in vocal prayer, realizing that you are in his presence.

The Samaritan woman asked Jesus for "living water." What do you desire from him? Begin by praying aloud these verses from Psalm 42:2–3 as your own. Then, continue expressing your desires to Jesus in your own words.

> ² As the deer longs for streams of water,
>   so my soul longs for you, [Jesus].
> ³ My soul thirsts for [you, Jesus], the living [water].
>   When can I enter and see [your face]?

After expressing your desires, prepare your heart for an encounter with Jesus in contemplative prayer.

Contemplation

As you pray contemplatively with this story of the woman at the well, engage your mind, heart, imagination, emotions, and all your senses. In your imagination, identify with the Samaritan woman. Allow the Holy Spirit to lead you into an intimate conversation with Jesus.

Place yourself in the gospel scene, standing in the place of the woman. Every time the story refers to the woman, personalize it with "I" or "me." For example, "I came to draw water. . . . Jesus said to me. . . ."

You see Jesus approaching you. What unworthiness keeps you from wanting to look at him?

Allow your gaze to meet Jesus's gaze. (Allow yourself to spend a few moments experiencing his gaze beholding you.) Describe the movements of your heart as you look at him and he looks at you.

Pay attention to how you feel internally as he comes close and asks you for a drink. How does this translate into your life? How might you satisfy his thirst?

Jesus then asks you if you would like "living water." How do you understand this "living water" that Jesus is offering you? How do you respond to his offer?

Now Jesus begins revealing your personal relational history. Pay attention to what you are experiencing as he reveals areas of your past and current broken relationships, showing you specific sins and wounds. (Ask the Holy Spirit to bring these areas of your personal history to mind now.)

When you think about these relationships, what were you desiring? How well were those desires fulfilled? How were they left unfulfilled?

Do you believe Jesus can and will satisfy your deepest desires? Why or why not?

What does it mean to you to worship in "Spirit and truth"? How does authentic worship fulfill you?

How does this encounter with Jesus motivate you to want to tell everyone about him? What do you want to tell them about Jesus?

Record your experience in this contemplative prayer in your prayer journal.

Action

Respond to your contemplative prayer experience with an action. Ask the Holy Spirit to inspire you.

Suggested Action: Spend some time going through your personal history of intimate relationships. Write down in your prayer journal the name of each person with whom you have had an intimate relationship. What were you desiring in each relationship? Then identify any ways you have sinned or been wounded in each of these relationships. Confess these sins in the Sacrament of Reconciliation, so you can experience Jesus's merciful gaze. If you do not have access to the Sacrament of Reconciliation, confess them to a trusted friend who will be able to respond with Jesus's love and mercy. Make eye contact.

Allow their loving gaze to heal you of your shame. If it seems prudent and for their good, contact any people you have hurt, and humbly apologize to them for specific ways you hurt them. Forgive others for any ways they have hurt you.

Alternative Action: If the suggested action does not fit you, ask the Holy Spirit to inspire an action that does.

WISDOM FROM THE CHURCH
As you reflect on Day 1, allow the wisdom from the Church to strengthen you in the graces of this day.

The Samaritan woman desired fulfillment in her broken human relationships, but she couldn't satisfy her deepest desires until she met Jesus. St. John Paul II in his 2000 World Youth Day address spoke about our universal longing for fulfillment: "It is Jesus in fact that you seek when you dream of happiness; He is waiting for you when nothing else you find satisfies you; He is the beauty to which you are so attracted; it is He who provoked you with that thirst for fullness that will not let you settle for compromise" (Pope John Paul II, "15th World Youth Day Address, Vigil of Prayer," 5). Just as in the Samaritan woman's case, it is Jesus who fulfills our deepest longings.

Like the Samaritan woman, we all have a battle going on in our hearts between desire and shame. In his *Theology of the Body*, John Paul II speaks of this battle as a turning of our desires away from the Father to the world: "The human heart holds within itself at one and the same time desire and shame. The birth of shame orients us toward the moment in which the inner man, 'the heart,' by closing itself to what 'comes from the Father' opens itself to what comes from the world.' The birth of shame in the human heart goes hand in hand with the beginning of concupiscence."[1] We too experience shame with our sin, but Jesus offers us healing.

Our healing comes when we fix our eyes on Jesus in contemplation and allow our hearts to be penetrated by his loving gaze, as the Samaritan woman did. The *Catechism* says: "Contemplation is a *gaze* of faith, fixed on Jesus. 'I look at him and he looks at me.' ... His gaze purifies our heart; the light of the countenance of Jesus illumines the eyes of our heart and teaches us to see everything in the light of his truth and his compassion for all men" (*CCC*, 2715).

FURTHER GROWTH

If you desire to explore this gospel passage and the theme in more depth, here are a few suggestions for further growth.

1. Read the preface and introduction of *Be Healed* (Ave Maria Press, 2014).

2. Watch a dramatization of this gospel scene in the video "Jesus and the Samaritan Woman at the Well" in the YouTube series *The Chosen* (season 1, episode 8) (*The Chosen*, 2020).

3. Read *The Journey of Desire* by John Eldridge (Thomas Nelson, 2000).

4. Listen to the song "Reckless Love" by Cory Asbury (Bethel Music, 2018).

5. Read *The Fulfillment of All Desire* by Ralph Martin (St. Paul Center / Emmaus Road, 2006).

"DO YOU WANT TO BE WELL?"

Rekindling Our Hope: Jesus and the Man at the Pool of Bethesda

John 5:1–15
(Based on Chapter 1 of *Be Healed*)

PREPARATION

Place yourself in the presence of God.

In the gospel account for today, we find Jesus encountering the disabled man at the pool of Bethesda. We are challenged to examine areas where we have suffered for a long time and may have lost hope that we can be healed. This hopelessness may originate in our reaction to our afflictions. Whenever we are faced with long-term sickness, emotional pain, or chronic sin, we may become discouraged. But we have a choice: we can remain in self-absorption or turn toward God for help. In her wisdom, the Church reminds us that these moments of anguish and hopelessness can be chances to search for and choose God: "Illness can lead to anguish, self-absorption, sometimes even despair and revolt against God. . . . Very often illness provokes a search for God and a return to him" (*CCC*, 1501).

LECTIO DIVINA
Gospel of John (5:1–15): Jesus Encounters the Man at the Pool of Bethesda

Take a few deep breaths. As you breathe, invite the Holy Spirit to inspire you as you pray with this scripture passage.

Reading

As you read through this gospel account, pay attention to the overall condition of the man by the pool (physically, psychologically, and spiritually). Attend to the details of the story. How long has he been suffering? How do you think he feels? Why do you think Jesus comes to him and not to the others? Notice how Jesus relates to this man. What does Jesus ask him? How does the man respond? Why do you think Jesus warns him not to sin when he meets him the second time?

After this, there was a feast of the Jews, and Jesus went up to Jerusalem. ² Now there is in Jerusalem at the Sheep [Gate] a pool called in Hebrew Bethesda, with five porticoes. ³ In these lay a large number of ill, blind, lame, and crippled. [⁴] ⁵ One man was there who had been ill for thirty-eight years. ⁶ When Jesus saw him lying there and knew that he had been ill for a long time, he said to him, "Do you want to be well?" ⁷ The sick man answered him, "Sir, I have no one to put me into the pool when the water is stirred up; while I am on my way, someone else gets down there before me." ⁸ Jesus said to him, "Rise, take up your mat, and walk." ⁹ Immediately the man became well, took up his mat, and walked.

Now that day was a sabbath. ¹⁰ So the Jews said to the man who was cured, "It is the sabbath, and it is not lawful for you to carry your mat." ¹¹ He answered them, "The man who made me well told me, 'Take up your mat and walk.'" ¹² They asked him, "Who is the man who told you, 'Take it up and walk'?" ¹³ The man who was healed did not know who it was, for Jesus had slipped away, since there was a crowd there. ¹⁴ After this Jesus found him in the temple area and said to him, "Look, you are well; do not sin any more, so

that nothing worse may happen to you." [15] The man
went and told the Jews that Jesus was the one who
had made him well.

Meditation

I am in awe at Jesus's insight into human nature. I know
he created us, but still his ability to see right into the
heart of a situation always amazes me. No matter how
badly bound we are, he seems to know the exact key to
unlock our prison doors. His encounter with the man
at the pool of Bethesda is a prime example.

Can you fathom what it was like for this lame man
to lay beside a "healing" pool for thirty-eight years but
never get in? To put it into a modern context, imagine
someone lying beside the healing waters of Lourdes for
thirty-eight years. Can you even imagine that? Day after
day, year after year, this man of Bethesda waited help-
lessly for someone to assist him. Thousands passed him
by until Jesus stopped and listened to the cry of his heart.

I'm sure Jesus approached this poor man with compassion, but I must admit, I'm a bit troubled by his opening words: "Do you want to be well?" (Jn 5:6). To me, it
sounds like Jesus is accusing him of playing the victim.
My initial reaction is to step in to defend this helpless
man. *Of course he wants to be healed. Look how long*

he has been suffering. But then, coming to my senses, I realize this is Jesus whom I am questioning. He must know something about the deeper paralysis of this man's soul that isn't immediately obvious to me. After all these years, it appears this lame man has given up hope that he will ever be healed. Who could blame him? Why hold on to hope, only to be disappointed again and again?

The longer I ponder Jesus's question to this man, the more I begin to feel a bit uneasy myself. He is not just asking this lame man if he wants to be healed. His question is directed to me and to you as well. After all these years of struggling with our various physical, psychological, and spiritual infirmities, have we somehow resigned ourselves to our broken condition, believing "this is as good as life gets"? Have we also given in to hopelessness, believing we won't be healed? Most of the time we aren't even aware of our resignation. We just accept our condition and bear it as best as we can. Can you relate?

As we move from focusing on the man of Bethesda who suffered for thirty-eight years to exploring our own ongoing afflictions, I invite you to take an honest look at how you have resigned yourself to your infirmities and given in to hopelessness. Realize that you are not alone in what you feel. The psalmist expresses this hopelessness to God on our behalf.

Vocal Prayer

Bring your personal areas of hopelessness, where you haven't yet been healed, to the Father in vocal prayer.

The man at the pool of Bethesda said: "There is no one to help me." The following prayer from Psalm 22:2–3 expresses the helplessness and hopelessness that we feel when we call out to God and don't receive an answer or get relief. Jesus himself prayed this psalm out loud from the Cross. Pray it aloud with him:

> ² My God, my God, why have you abandoned me?
>   Why so far from my call for help,
>   from my cries of anguish?
> ³ My God, I call by day, but you do not answer;
>   by night, but I have no relief.

Think of an area where you have called out to God and have not yet received healing. Continue in your own words expressing to God your discouragement over not yet being healed of your affliction. Don't be afraid to be real with God. If it is acceptable for Jesus to speak this way to the Father, it is acceptable for you as well.

After expressing your feelings to God, bring these areas of discouragement and longing into the following contemplative prayer experience.

Contemplation

*Return to the gospel passage and place yourself in the story as the man who has been disabled there for thirty-eight years. Feel his anguish. Use personal pronouns in the dialogue with Jesus. For example, "When Jesus **saw me** lying there and knew that **I** had been ill for a long time, **he asked me**, "Do you want to be well?"*

Assume a comfortable position and take a few deep breaths.

Pray, "Come, Holy Spirit."

Ask the Holy Spirit to show you an area of your life (physically, psychologically, or spiritually) where you have been suffering for a long time and have felt helpless and hopeless.

Consider all the futile efforts you have attempted over the years to be healed of this affliction.

Allow yourself to feel your helplessness and hopelessness in the situation. In this helpless and hopeless condition, what do you believe about God? About life? About yourself? (Write these specific beliefs down in your prayer journal.)

As you are in touch with your helplessness and hopelessness, look up and see Jesus approaching you. (Take a moment to pay attention to your experience as he approaches.) How do you respond, realizing he is coming to you personally?

What do you experience when Jesus asks you the question: "Do you want to be well?" (Take a moment to pay attention to what you are thinking and feeling as he asks you this question.)

How do you answer Jesus's question? (Be honest with him and with yourself.)

How does Jesus answer you? What does he command you to do?

How do you respond to his command?

Imagine you are instantly healed when Jesus speaks these words to you. What does it feel like to be healed of your ailment? (Take a moment and allow yourself to experience how your life is different living without this affliction.)

How do you feel and respond when the people in authority interrogate you about your encounter with Jesus?

What is the area of sin that Jesus warns you about at the end?

If you are having difficulty getting past your feelings of helplessness and hopelessness, pray this out loud: "In the name of Jesus Christ, I renounce the lie that things will never change and that I will never be healed. I renounce the belief that I am a helpless victim with no one to help me. I

announce the truth that Jesus's power is made perfect in my
weakness (see 2 Corinthians 12:9). I announce the truth that
Jesus is my healer and savior (see Ephesians 1:6).

Write down your thoughts, feelings, and desires in your
prayer journal.

Action

*Respond to your contemplative prayer experience with an
action.*

Suggested Action: Ask the Holy Spirit to show you an
area where you have given into sloth, physically, emotionally, or spiritually. Make a determined commitment
to act deliberately in this area, so that you can live with
greater charity.

Alternative Action: If the suggested action does not fit
you, ask the Holy Spirit to inspire an action that does.

WISDOM FROM THE CHURCH

*As you reflect on Day 2, allow the wisdom from the Church
to help you strengthen the graces of this day.*

Often disguised behind our hopelessness is a certain kind of presumption and self-reliance. The Church
reminds us to choose humility and trust in these

moments instead: "Painful as discouragement is, it is the reverse of presumption. The humble are not surprised by their distress; it leads them to trust more, to hold fast in constancy" (*CCC*, 2733). When we are humble, we acknowledge our need for Jesus.

The Church believes that Jesus is our Divine Physician. He came to heal us and commanded the Church to carry out this work: "'Heal the sick!' The Church has received this charge from the Lord and strives to carry it out. . . . She believes in the life-giving presence of Christ, the physician of souls and bodies" (*CCC*, 1509).

Healing, in fact, is one of the ways we come to believe that God is near and that he has compassion for our suffering: "Christ's compassion toward the sick and his many healings of every kind of infirmity are a resplendent sign that 'God has visited his people' and that the Kingdom of God is close at hand" (*CCC*, 1503). "Often Jesus asks the sick to believe" (*CCC*, 1504). Encouraging faith and trust, Jesus offers hope to the hopeless.

FURTHER GROWTH

If you desire to explore this gospel passage and the theme in more depth, here are a few suggestions for further growth.

1. Read chapter 1 of *Be Healed* (Ave Maria Press, 2014).

2. Watch a dramatization of this gospel scene in the video "Jesus Heals Paralytic at Pool of Bethesda" in the YouTube series *The Chosen* (season 2, episode 4) (*The Chosen*, 2021).

3. Read *Healing: Bringing the Gift of God's Mercy to the World* by Mary Healy (Our Sunday Visitor, 2015).

4. Listen to the song "Oceans" by Hillsong (2013).

5. Read *Unbound: A Practical Guide to Deliverance from Evil Spirits* by Neal Lozano (Chosen Books, 2010).

DAY 3

"WHY DO YOU CALL ME GOOD?"

Prioritizing Pure Love: Jesus and the Rich Official

Luke 18:18–30
(Based on Chapter 2 of *Be Healed*)

PREPARATION

Place yourself in the presence of God.

In reflecting on the encounter between Jesus and the rich official in Luke's gospel, we are challenged to examine our understanding of goodness and the way to eternal life. Do we love Jesus above everything and everyone else? (see Revelation 2:4). Commenting on this gospel passage, St. John Paul II observes: "The question which the Rich young man puts to Jesus of Nazareth is one which arises from the depths of his heart. It is *an essential and unavoidable question for the life of every man,* for it is about the moral good which must be done, and about eternal life. . . . *To ask about the good,* in fact, *ultimately means to turn towards God,* the fullness of goodness" (*Veritatis Splendor,* 8–9).

▌ LECTIO DIVINA
Gospel of Luke (18:18–30):
Jesus Encounters the Rich Official

Take a few deep breaths. As you breathe, invite the Holy Spirit to inspire you as you pray with this scripture passage.

Reading
Slowly read through this gospel account and make note of the rich official's earnest desire for eternal life. Notice his obedience in keeping the commandments, as well as his reluctance to part with his wealth and social status. Why do you think Jesus challenged him with the question "Why do you call me good?" and then responded, "No one is good but God alone"? Was Jesus denying his own goodness or divinity? How does this man respond when Jesus tells him to sell everything and give it to the poor? Notice the contrast between this man, who chose not to follow Jesus, and the disciples, who have given up everything to follow Jesus.

[18] An official asked him this question, "Good teacher, what must I do to inherit eternal life?" [19] Jesus answered him, "Why do you call me good? No one is good but God alone. [20] You know the commandments, 'You shall not commit adultery; you shall not kill; you shall not steal; you shall not bear false witness; honor your father and your mother.'" [21] And he replied, "All of these I have observed from my youth." [22] When Jesus heard this he said to him, "There is still one thing left for you: sell all that you have and distribute it to the poor, and you will have a treasure in heaven. Then come, follow me." [23] But when he heard this he became quite sad, for he was very rich.

[24] Jesus looked at him [now sad] and said, "How hard it is for those who have wealth to enter the kingdom of God! [25] For it is easier for a camel to pass through the eye of a needle than for a rich person to enter the kingdom of God." [26] Those who heard this said, "Then who can be saved?" [27] And he said, "What is impossible for human beings is possible for God." [28] Then Peter said, "We have given up our possessions and followed you." [29] He said to them, "Amen, I say to you, there is no one who has given up house or wife or brothers or parents or children for the sake of the

kingdom of God [30] who will not receive [back] an over-abundant return in this present age and eternal life in the age to come."

Meditation

Jesus didn't have casual students; he had disciples who gave up everything to follow him. They believed in him with their entire lives and followed him everywhere he went. They didn't just sit in school and study to acquire knowledge. They followed Jesus and did everything he did.

I began to comprehend that believing in Jesus was much more than reciting the creed, keeping the commandments, or going to church on Sunday. It required a radical commitment of my life and everything associated with it. Jesus's dialogue with the rich official in Luke's gospel made this abundantly clear. Jesus saw this man's genuine goodness and admired him. But he wanted to take away any grounds for this man's self-righteousness or self-reliance, showing that God is the source and origin of all true goodness and that genuine faith requires a radical dependence on God and not on one's self. Jesus is the only good teacher because he is God; he alone is truly good. Otherwise, he would have no authority to call this man or any of us to such radical discipleship.

Following Jesus sounds attractive, until we have to give up our self-sufficiency. Aren't we all terrified at some level when we read this story? We try to rationalize it away; does Jesus really require us to let go of everything in order to follow him? Can you relate, or am I the only one who finds this frightening? I am consoled that Pope Francis understands my fear. When teaching on the Beatitudes, he said, "We are afraid of salvation. We need it, but we are afraid. We have to give everything. He is in charge! And we are afraid of this . . . we want control of ourselves."[2]

The rich official knew and obeyed the commandments from his youth. By any standard in his culture and ours, he would be considered a "good man." Everything about him was exemplary. He was honest and just. He was faithful to his wife and respectful to his neighbors. He was obedient to God and to his parents. He was wealthy, but not through dishonest gain. He had status and influence, which he bore with honor. But despite this, Jesus challenged him to let go of his reliance on his wealth and his own righteousness. Jesus was inviting him to a much greater good and much greater wealth— an adventurous relationship with the living God as a disciple of Jesus.

The rich official knew the value of a good return on investment and was actively seeking what Jesus promised—eternal life. But he turned away sad, because he refused to let go of his attachments and his ungodly self-reliance. Is some of our own sadness, perhaps, due to the same thing? We live on our own terms and want to be good in our own eyes, yet we feel emptiness. When we seek to preserve our own life, we lose the very essence of life itself. Are we ready to let go of our false securities to discover our lasting inheritance, which will bring us true joy? Peter and the other disciples knew what it was like to give up everything to follow Jesus. In return, Jesus promised them an even greater inheritance in this life and "eternal life in the age to come."

Vocal Prayer

If you desire to follow Jesus, speak directly to him in vocal prayer.

The following prayer is from Psalm 25:4–5. Begin by praying it aloud:

⁴ Make known to me your ways, LORD;
    teach me your paths.
⁵ Guide me by your fidelity and teach me,
    for you are God my savior,
    for you I wait all the day long.

Continue praying in your own words, praising God for his goodness and expressing your trust that he has good things for you. Speak to him about your fears of letting go of your earthly securities to have eternal security in him.

After expressing your desires, prepare your heart for an encounter with Jesus in contemplative prayer.

Contemplation

*I invite you in to bring your fears of letting go of your attachments to Jesus in this contemplative prayer. Identifying with the rich official, place yourself in the scene of the gospel. Allow the Holy Spirit to guide your imagination as you encounter Jesus in this prayer experience. Every time the story refers to the rich official, replace his name with a personal pronoun—for example, "**I** went up to Jesus and asked him a question, 'What must I do to inherit eternal life?'"*

Assume a comfortable position and take a few deep breaths. Pray, "Come, Holy Spirit."

Become aware of your desires to live a virtuous life, to please God, and to have eternal life.

What are some of the good things you have done in your life that you can tell Jesus about?

In what ways are you wealthy—materially, relationally, and spiritually?

Can you identify any areas of self-reliance or self-righ-teousness where you have trusted in your possessions, virtues, or abilities?

You are face-to-face with Jesus. You say to him: "Good Teacher, what must I do to inherit eternal life?"

What is your reaction to Jesus's response: "Why do you call me good? No one is good but God alone."

When he tells you to keep the commandments, what is your answer to him? Have you kept them as well as the rich official? Have you kept them as well as Jesus?

Ask the Holy Spirit to show you any specific attachments that get in the way of your relationship with Jesus.

You are face-to-face with Jesus in personal conversation. He looks at you with love and asks you to let go of these attachments that prevent you from following him whole-heartedly. Acknowledge your fears as he asks you this. How do you respond?

What are you not willing to let go of to follow Jesus more fully? Allow yourself to feel the sorrow of the loss of intimacy with Jesus as you hold on to your attachments as a security blanket.

Then listen to Jesus's response to you. What do you experience?

Finally imagine yourself in the place of Peter, telling Jesus: "Lord, I have given up everything to follow you." Pay attention to the experience of giving up everything to follow Jesus. Describe what you are feeling.

What does Jesus promise you? What is your response to his promise?

Record your reflection in your prayer journal. What is your overall experience in this encounter with Jesus?

Action

Respond to your contemplative prayer experience with an action. Pray and ask the Holy Spirit to inspire you.

Suggested Action: As you identify an area of earthly attachment that is hindering your relationship with Jesus, take a step of faith by renouncing that attachment. Then demonstrate your renouncement with an action that demonstrates it. For example, if you are attached to money or financial security, give beyond your comfort level. Or if you are attached to approval or status, decide to "take the lowest place" and go unnoticed over the next week.

Alternative Action: If the suggested action does not fit you, ask the Holy Spirit to inspire an action that does.

WISDOM FROM THE CHURCH

As you reflect on Day 3, allow the wisdom from the Church to help you strengthen the graces of this day.

The rich official was divided in his desires. He wanted to do good and to love God, but he also wanted to hold on to his possessions, positions, and prestige. The Second Vatican Council in its document *Gaudium et Spes (On the Church in the Modern World)* speaks about this same battle in each of our souls: "Man is divided in himself. As a result, the whole life of men, both individual and social, shows itself to be a struggle, and a dramatic one, between good and evil, between light and darkness"(13).

As he did with the rich official, Jesus calls us to let go of anything that prevents us from following him with our whole heart. "Jesus enjoins his disciples to prefer him to everything and everyone, and bids them 'renounce all that [they have]' for his sake and that of the Gospel. . . . The precept of detachment from riches is obligatory for entrance into the Kingdom of heaven" (*CCC*, 2544). We are all called to value spiritual riches more than things of this world.

To grow closer to Jesus, we need to choose the way of the Cross: "Spiritual progress tends toward ever more intimate union with Christ" (*CCC*, 2014). "The way of perfection passes by way of the Cross. There is no holiness without renunciation and spiritual battle" (*CCC*, 2015). Loving sacrifice leads us to a closer relationship with Jesus.

FURTHER GROWTH

If you desire to explore this gospel passage and the theme in more depth, here are a few suggestions for further growth.

1. Read chapter 2 of *Be Healed* (Ave Maria Press, 2014).

2. Watch the video "The Rich Young Ruler" on You-Tube (Open Bible Stories, 2015).

3. Read *St. Francis of Assisi* by G. K. Chesterton (Paraclete Press, 2013).

4. Listen to the song "Nothing I Hold Onto" by Will Reagan (2010).

5. Read *Always Enough: God's Miraculous Provision Among the Poorest Children on Earth* by Roland and Heidi Baker (Chosen Books, 2003).

"DO YOU BELIEVE THAT I CAN DO THIS?"

Restoring Our Faith: Jesus and the Two Blind Men

Matthew 9:27–31, 35–38
(Based on Chapter 3 of *Be Healed*)

PREPARATION

Place yourself in the presence of God.

Jesus's encounter with the two blind men in the Gospel of Matthew shows us his compassion for their plight as well as the boldness of their faith. It also underscores Jesus's deep concern for all of us who are like "sheep without a shepherd" until he becomes our Good Shepherd. The story invites us to examine our own faith as

we acknowledge areas of our spiritual blindness and
dependence on God.

Though we may be blind to many things, we are
all in need of God's mercy. Jesus responds to our plea:
"The urgent request of the blind men, 'Have mercy on
us, Son of David' or 'Jesus, Son of David, have mercy
on me!' has been renewed in the traditional prayer to
Jesus known as the *Jesus Prayer*: "Lord Jesus Christ, son
of God, have mercy on me, a sinner!" Healing infirmities or forgiving sins, Jesus always responds to a prayer
offered in faith: 'Your faith has made you well; go in
peace" (*CCC*, 2616).

LECTIO DIVINA
Gospel of Matthew (9:27–31, 35–38):
Jesus Encounters Two Blind Men

*Take a few deep breaths. As you breathe, invite the Holy
Spirit to inspire you as you pray with this scripture passage.*

Reading
*As you read slowly through this gospel account, pay atten-
tion to the question that Jesus asks the two blind men.
Notice the simple confidence they have in Jesus. Though
they are blind, they see what most of the religious leaders*

do not—Jesus's identity as well as his compassion for suffering humanity. We are called to see what Jesus sees—the needs of the people around us as well as our own needs—and then come to him in bold faith.

[27] As Jesus passed on from there, two blind men followed [him], crying out, "Son of David, have pity on us!" [28] When he entered the house, the blind men approached him and Jesus said to them, "Do you believe that I can do this?" "Yes, Lord," they said to him. [29] Then he touched their eyes and said, "Let it be done for you according to your faith." [30] And their eyes were opened. Jesus warned them sternly, "See that no one knows about this." [31] But they went out and spread word of him through all that land.

[35] Jesus went around to all the towns and villages, teaching in their synagogues, proclaiming the gospel of the kingdom, and curing every disease and illness. [36] At the sight of the crowds, his heart was moved with pity for them because they were troubled and abandoned, like sheep without a shepherd. [37] Then he said to his disciples, "The harvest is abundant but the laborers are few; [38] so ask the master of the harvest to send out laborers for his harvest."

Meditation

Stepping into the gospel story of Matthew 9:27, imagine that you and I are the two blind people who seek an encounter with Jesus. You and I whisper to each other, "Maybe he will heal us." It seems impossible, but news of a paralyzed man being cured in the next village buoys our hopes even more. Our sense of anticipation rises as reports that the healer is heading our way spreads through our village. All around us we hear the buzzing of the crowd. They say he is somewhere on the road in front of us. We stumble along behind the multitude, shouting, "Son of David, have pity on us!" Without warning, the crowd stops abruptly in front of someone's house. The healer has disappeared. Is he inside? Have we missed our chance? Undeterred, we cry out again, with even greater fervor, "Son of David, have pity on us!" Confident that he hears us, we instinctively quiet ourselves, waiting, hoping that he does not pass us by. For once we *want* to be noticed.

A voice responds from inside the house; the Healer has acknowledged our plea and is coming out to meet us. Within seconds we feel his presence standing directly in front of us. We hold our breath, as he gently reaches out his hand to touch our eyes; his few words bear an unmistakable authority, and the kindness in his voice pierces our hearts in a way we've never experienced. We feel loved and know by this man, who seconds ago was just a stranger.

As he touches our eyes, we feel power flowing from his hands and warmth spreading out throughout our bodies. Our eyes flutter and begin to tingle. Suddenly light flashes in front of us, like the lightning bolts that light up the sky in the middle of a summer storm. Within seconds, tears of gratitude pour down our cheeks like torrents of rain. When the clearing comes, we can *see*. Faces all around us are astonished, mirroring our own amazement. Who is this man, and who besides the mighty Elijah has ever restored the sight of ones born blind?

Shocked, we try to make sense of what is happening. Our eyes are drawn to meet the gaze of the Healer. He sees *us*. For some unknown reason, we matter to this man. He treats us with a reverence we have never seen before; it is almost too much to bear. Without words, his gentle eyes communicate a desire to heal our entire being. Our physical healing, astonishing as it is, pales in comparison to the healing he now offers us. Without words he speaks to the depths of our hearts. His penetrating gaze says it all, offering to restore all those areas of our souls that have been blinded by pride, fear, and unbelief.

Vocal Prayer

Acknowledging that we all have been blinded by areas of pride, fear, and unbelief, let us turn to Jesus in vocal prayer, asking him to restore our vision.

The following prayer is from Psalm 27:7–8. Pray it aloud. Then continue in your own words, asking Jesus to have mercy on you and answer you in your need.

> [7] Hear my voice, LORD, when I call;
>   have mercy on me and answer.
> [8] "Come," says my heart, "seek his face";
>   your face, LORD, do I seek!

As you finish expressing your needs to Jesus, quiet your mind and prepare your heart for an encounter with Jesus in the following contemplative prayer.

Contemplation

As you pray contemplatively with this scripture passage, continue identifying with one of the two blind people. Allow the Holy Spirit to guide you as you encounter Jesus in this prayer experience. Every time the story refers to the blind men, place yourself in the story—for example, "**We** followed Jesus and cried out, 'Son of David, have pity **on us**!'" (or "**I** followed Jesus and cried out, 'Son of David, have pity on **me**!'").

Get in a comfortable position and take a few deep breaths. Pray, "Come, Holy Spirit."

We are all spiritually blind in some ways. Ask the Holy Spirit to reveal to you an area of your own spiritual blindness. (It may be blindness to spiritual truths; blindness to your own sin; blindness to Jesus's presence with you; blindness to the needs of family members; blindness to the poor in your community; or any other area of your life where you don't see with God's eyes.)

Become aware of your desires. What do you want Jesus to do for you?

In touch with the depth of your desires, cry out loudly: "Jesus, Son of David, have pity on me!"

What area of your life are you asking him to heal? What pride, fear, unbelief, or judgment keeps you from seeing Jesus and other people with God's vision?

Your prayer is both for yourself and for those you are journeying with. What do you want to see? What do you desire for those in your house or community to see?

Jesus asks you, "Do you believe that I can do this for you?" How do you respond?

Allow yourself to feel Jesus's compassion, in the way he touches you and speaks to you. Feel the power coming through his hands and the confident authority in his voice. (Allow yourself to experience this now, through the power of the Holy Spirit.)

As Jesus heals you in this area of spiritual blindness, what do you see?

Describe your experience and insights in your prayer journal.

What action flows from your restored vision?

Action

Respond to your contemplative prayer experience with an action. Ask the Holy Spirit to inspire you.

Suggested Action: Spend some time in prayer asking the Father to show you areas where you doubt his power to heal or have been blind to your own needs and the needs of others around you. Ask him to open your eyes to see the "sheep without a shepherd" in your surroundings. It could be within yourself, family members, people in your community, or people with special needs that you feel compassion toward. Then begin daily interceding for these people, asking the "master of the harvest to send out laborers for his harvest." If you feel called to it, follow your time of prayer with an act of service for them.

Alternative Action: Read one of the books below to stretch your faith in Jesus's power to heal.

WISDOM FROM THE CHURCH

As you reflect on Day 4, allow the wisdom from the Church to help you strengthen the graces of this day.

We are all spiritually blind in some way. The Church exhorts us to recognize the various sources of our spiritual blindness and the danger to our souls when we stubbornly refuse to believe in God's presence and power: "*Voluntary doubt* about the faith disregards or refuses to hold true what God has revealed and the Church proposes for belief. *Involuntary doubt* refers to hesitation in believing, difficulty in overcoming objections connected to the faith, or also anxiety aroused by its obscurity. If deliberately cultivated *doubt can lead to spiritual blindness*" (*CCC*, 2088, last emphasis added).

Because of their faith in Jesus, the two blind men were able to see what others could not see. As we allow the Holy Spirit to purify our hearts, we are enabled to see God more clearly in every situation and in every person we encounter: "The 'pure in heart' are promised that they will see God face to face and be like him. Purity of heart is the precondition of the vision of God. Even now it enables us to see *according* to God, to accept others as "neighbors"; it lets us perceive the human body—ours and our neighbor's—as a temple of the Holy Spirit, a manifestation of divine beauty" (*CCC*, 2519).

The two blind men in the Gospel of Matthew had interior vision that allowed them to see and believe in Jesus within their hearts before they could see him with their eyes. The Church encourages contemplation as a way for all of us to purify our hearts so that we can see Jesus more clearly: "Contemplation is a *gaze* of faith, fixed on Jesus. . . . His gaze purifies our heart; the light of the countenance of Jesus illumines the eyes of our heart and teaches us to see everything in the light of his truth and his compassion for all men" (*CCC*, 2715). Through contemplative prayer, our faith and our spiritual vision is strengthened.

FURTHER GROWTH

If you desire to explore this gospel passage and the theme in more depth, here are a few suggestions for further growth.

1. Read chapter 3 of *Be Healed* (Ave Maria Press, 2014).

2. Watch the video "Jesus, Healing of the Blind Beggar, Bartimaeus" on YouTube (Jesus Film, 2011).

3. Read *Open My Eyes, Lord: A Practical Guide to Angelic Visitations and Heavenly Experiences* by Gary Oates (Open Heaven, 2005).

4. Listen to the song "Lord, I Need You" by Matt Maher (2013).

5. Read *Lord, Renew Your Wonders: Spiritual Gifts for Today* by Damian Stayne (Word Among Us Press, 2017).

"DO YOU KNOW THE FATHER'S LOVE?"

Reclaiming Our Inheritance:
Jesus Tells the Parable of Two Sons

Luke 15:11–32
(Based on Chapter 4 of *Be Healed*)

PREPARATION

Place yourself in the presence of God.

Jesus lived constantly in the knowledge of his Father's love, confident in his identity as Beloved Son. But he had repeated encounters with people of every social status, including religious leaders and outcasts in society, who did not know they were beloved sons and daughters of the Father. The story of the prodigal son, in Luke's gospel, was intended to show the Father's merciful heart for all people. This story invites us to examine how we see ourselves as sons (and daughters) of our heavenly Father. No matter what we have done or failed to do, our Father invites us to receive his merciful love and be affirmed in our identity as his beloved one.

In his homily for World Youth Day Mass in 2002, St. John Paul II reminded all of us of this truth: "We are not the sum of our weaknesses and failures; we are the sum of the Father's love for us and our real capacity to become the image of the Son" (5).

LECTIO DIVINA
Gospel of Luke (15:11–32): Jesus Tells the Story of the Father with His Two Sons

Take a few deep breaths. As you breathe, invite the Holy Spirit to inspire you as you pray with this scripture passage.

Reading

As you read slowly through this gospel account, pay attention to the differences between the two sons. With which of these two sons do you most identify? Can you identify with each of them in some way? Notice how the father in the story relates to each of them uniquely. What images and phrases in the story speak to your heart?

[11] [Jesus] said, "A man had two sons, [12] and the younger son said to his father, 'Father, give me the share of your estate that should come to me.' So the father divided the property between them. [13] After a few days, the younger son collected all his belongings and set off to a distant country where he squandered his inheritance on a life of dissipation. [14] When he had freely spent everything, a severe famine struck that country, and he found himself in dire need. [15] So he hired himself out to one of the local citizens who sent him to his farm to tend the swine. [16] And he longed to eat his fill of the pods on which the swine fed, but nobody gave him any. [17] Coming to his senses he thought, 'How many of my father's hired workers have more than enough food to eat, but here am I, dying from hunger. [18] I shall get up and go to my father and I shall say to him, "Father, I have sinned against heaven and against you. [19] I no longer deserve to be called your son; treat me as you would treat one of your hired workers."' [20] So he got up and went back to his father. While he was still a long way off, his father caught sight of him, and was filled with compassion. He ran to his son, embraced him and kissed him. [21] His son said to him, 'Father, I have sinned against heaven and against you; I no longer deserve

to be called your son.' [22] But his father ordered his servants, 'Quickly bring the finest robe and put it on him; put a ring on his finger and sandals on his feet. [23] Take the fattened calf and slaughter it. Then let us celebrate with a feast, [24] because this son of mine was dead, and has come to life again; he was lost, and has been found.' Then the celebration began. [25] Now the older son had been out in the field and, on his way back, as he neared the house, he heard the sound of music and dancing. [26] He called one of the servants and asked what this might mean. [27] The servant said to him, 'Your brother has returned and your father has slaughtered the fattened calf because he has him back safe and sound.' [28] He became angry, and when he refused to enter the house, his father came out and pleaded with him. [29] He said to his father in reply, 'Look, all these years I served you and not once did I disobey your orders; yet you never gave me even a young goat to feast on with my friends. [30] But when your son returns who swallowed up your property with prostitutes, for him you slaughter the fattened calf.' [31] He said to him, 'My son, you are here with me always; everything I have is yours. [32] But now we must celebrate and rejoice, because your brother was dead and has come to life again; he was lost and has been found.'"

Meditation

The prodigal son parable shows the depth of the Father's love for each one of us. When we received a *spirit of adoption* at our baptisms, we were promised boundless treasures from the Father's storehouse. Jesus said all we have to do is ask because the Father delights in giving us good gifts (see Luke 11:13). When we trust him, we can bring our desires and brokenness to the Father and allow ourselves to become vulnerable enough to receive the healing we need in our lives. In contrast, when we do not believe that we are the Father's beloved, we remain bound in a *spirit of slavery* (see Romans 8:15) borne out of fear. Rather than living in freedom and communion with Jesus, we spend our days under the constant oppression of sin and law.

We become like one or both of the sons in Jesus's parable of the prodigal son. We either wind up like the older brother, who keeps trying to earn his Father's love and looks down on his brother, or we wind up as the younger one, who gives up trying to please the Father and indulges in a life of sin. Most of us start our healing journey identifying more with one son or the other.

Which of the two sons do you relate to the most? Are you more like the dutiful son, trying to please the Father by being good enough to get his approval? Or are you more like the rebellious son, choosing instead to indulge in whatever will medicate your pain? Either way, trying to find life apart from the Father leaves us miserable and acting like orphans who have to beg for spiritual food.[3] We have nowhere to go with our pain and unmet needs. Without a firm identity as beloved children, we end up living lives of moral perfectionism, trying to please God, or of reckless abandon and self-indulgence.

In Henri Nouwen's brilliant reflection on the prodigal son story, he discovered elements of both sons in himself and invites us to do the same.[4] As our eyes are opened to face our brokenness, we too become aware that we can identify with both sons. They have much in common. Both remain blinded to the father's unconditional love for them. Neither realizes that the father is waiting with open arms to receive them. They both try to resolve their pain apart from the father. One (the older brother) covers his hurt with performance and hides his sins; the other relieves his pain with addictions. Whether we are "rebels" or "rule keepers," we cannot shake the shackles of pride and shame.

Underneath all our masks and escapes, both sons remain controlled by a servile fear of God, leading each to run away and hide from "God the taskmaster." Whether we outwardly thumb our nose at him or more respectively numb our hearts by constantly striving to please him, we will remain distant from him. As a child of God through baptism, you have permanent access to the Father. He has given you everything. And he sees you with the eyes of compassion. No matter whether you are a "rebel" or a "rule keeper," your Father is welcoming you with open arms.

Vocal Prayer

Call out to the Father in vocal prayer.

The following prayer is from Psalm 25:6–7. Pray it aloud. Then continue thanking the Father for his unconditional love and tender mercy.

⁶ Remember your compassion and your mercy, O
     LORD,
          for they are ages old.
⁷ Remember no more the sins of my youth;
          remember me according to your mercy,
     because of your goodness, LORD.

When you are ready, allow your gratitude to draw you to rest in the Father's loving embrace in contemplative prayer.

Contemplation

As you pray contemplatively with this scripture passage, begin by identifying with each son. (If you are a woman, you can change the "sons/brothers" to "daughters/sisters.") Allow the Holy Spirit to guide your imagination as you encounter the Father in this prayer experience.

*Every time the story refers to the two sons, place yourself in the story—for example, in verse 20: "So **I** got up and went back to **my** father. While **I** was still a long way off, **my** father caught sight of **me**, and was filled with compassion." Similarly in verse 28: "**I** became angry, and when **I** refused to enter the house, **my** father came out and pleaded with **me**."*

Get in a comfortable position and take a few deep breaths. Pray, "Come, Holy Spirit."

One at a time, imagine you are each of the two sons. . . .

Identifying with the younger son, ask the Holy Spirit to reveal to you an area of sin and rebellion, or self-indulgence, either in the present or earlier in your life.

Become aware of your desires. What is it you are really wanting, beneath the sinful self-indulgence?

Allow yourself to experience the emptiness of trying to satisfy that desire yourself, but never really being fulfilled by your repeated self-indulgence.

Feel your shame, and speak words to describe how you have internalized it into your identity: "I am (e.g., bad, dirty, stupid, unworthy . . .)."

Experience the moment when you say, "This isn't satisfying me," and then decide to return to your Father's house. What motivates you to go back to the Father?

What are you experiencing and saying to yourself as you head back toward your Father's house?

How do you feel when the Father runs out toward you and embraces you?

Listen to the Father's words as he greets you and orders his servants. How do you feel? What do you think?

What is it like to be in the Father's presence? To be washed? Given the finest robe? What do you experience at the feast in your honor? What does the ring signify to you?

What do you experience now that the Father has washed away your sins and restored you as his beloved son or daughter?

How do you feel, knowing that your older brother resents you?

(Now allow yourself to stand in the place of the older son to experience this from his side.)

What does it feel like to see your brother treat your Father with such disdain?

What do you experience while your brother is gone out into the far country, and you don't know where he is or what he is doing?

What do you experience when you see your brother come back and your Father run out to greet him?

What do you believe about your brother and your Father at that moment? Where is your mother? How do you imagine she is feeling through all of this?

When you see the celebration and honor your brother is getting, how do you feel?

What do you experience when your Father comes out and pleads with you to come in to celebrate?

Finally, spend some time contemplating this statement from your heavenly Father: "My son [or daughter], you are here with me always; everything I have is yours."

(If you would like to spend more time contemplating this parable, go back a third time and experience it in identification with the father.)

Write down your emotions and insights in your prayer journal.

Action

Respond to your contemplative prayer experience with an action. Ask the Holy Spirit to inspire you.

Suggested Action: Ask your father or mother, a spiritual mother or father, or your pastor (or someone else in spiritual authority) to pray a blessing over you, asking your heavenly Father to bless you and further reveal your identity as his beloved son or daughter.

Alternative Action: If the suggested action does not fit you, ask the Holy Spirit to inspire an action that does.

WISDOM FROM THE CHURCH

As you reflect on Day 5, allow the wisdom from the Church to help you strengthen the graces of this day.

St. John Paul II loved this parable of the prodigal son and referred to it often in different ways. In his encyclical *Dives in Misericordia (On the Mercy of God)*, he emphasizes the father's faithfulness to himself even when his sons are unfaithful in different ways: "The father of the prodigal son is faithful to his fatherhood, faithful to the love that he had always lavished on his son" (6).

The Church teaches that the Sacrament of Penance is a practical application of the parable of the prodigal son. Each time you go to Confession, imagine yourself being embraced and blessed by your heavenly Father: "When he celebrates the sacrament of Penance, the priest is fulfilling the ministry of . . . the Father who awaits the prodigal son and welcomes him on his return" (*CCC*, 1465).

Ultimately this parable of the prodigal son is a summation of our entire spiritual journey. It represents the central mission of the Church: "The ultimate purpose of mission is none other than to make men share in the communion between the Father and the Son in their Spirit of love" (*CCC*, 850).

FURTHER GROWTH

If you desire to explore this gospel passage and the theme in more depth, here are a few suggestions for further growth.

1. Read chapter 4 of *Be Healed* (Ave Maria Press, 2014).

2. Watch the video "The Parable of the Prodigal Son" on YouTube (Nazareth Village, 2015).

3. Read *The Return of the Prodigal Son: A Story of Homecoming* by Henri Nouwen (Image Books, 1994).

4. Listen to the song "Run to the Father" by Matt Maher (2020).

5. Read *The Older Brother Returns: Finding a Renewed Sense of God's Love and Mercy* by Neal Lozano (Attic Studio Press, 1995).

DAY 6

"WHAT ARE YOU THINKING IN YOUR HEART?"

Healing from the Inside Out:
Jesus and the Paralyzed Man

Luke 5:17–26
(Based on Chapters 5 and 6 of *Be Healed*)

PREPARATION

Place yourself in the presence of God.

In the encounter with the paralyzed man, Jesus is attentive to what is going on in the hearts of each person in the scene. He knows the condition of the paralyzed man's heart, as well that of his friends who brought him down through the roof. He also sees the motives in the hardened hearts of the Pharisees and teachers who are observing this miracle take place.

God alone knows our hearts: "The heart is our hidden center, beyond the grasp of our reason and of others; only the Spirit of God can fathom the human heart and know it fully" (*CCC*, 2563).

LECTIO DIVINA
Gospel of Luke (5:17–26): Jesus
Encounters the Paralyzed Man

Take a few deep breaths. As you breathe, invite the Holy Spirit to inspire you as you pray with this scripture passage.

Reading
As you read slowly through this gospel account, pay attention to the different groups of people present: Jesus (and most likely his disciples), the paralyzed man, his friends who brought him to Jesus, the Pharisees and teachers of the Law, and the astonished crowd. Notice the outward condition and status of each person. Then note how Jesus sees into the depths of their hearts. Observe that Jesus has a "whole-person perspective" and sees the underlying roots of each one's condition.

¹⁷ One day as Jesus was teaching, Pharisees and teachers of the law were sitting there who had come from

every village of Galilee and Judea and Jerusalem, and the power of the Lord was with him for healing. [18] And some men brought on a stretcher a man who was paralyzed; they were trying to bring him in and set [him] in his presence. [19] But not finding a way to bring him in because of the crowd, they went up on the roof and lowered him on the stretcher through the tiles into the middle in front of Jesus. [20] When he saw their faith, he said, "As for you, your sins are forgiven." [21] Then the scribes and Pharisees began to ask themselves, "Who is this who speaks blasphemies? Who but God alone can forgive sins?" [22] Jesus knew their thoughts and said to them in reply, "What are you thinking in your hearts? [23] Which is easier, to say, 'Your sins are forgiven,' or to say, 'Rise and walk'? [24] But that you may know that the Son of Man has authority on earth to forgive sins"— he said to the man who was paralyzed, "I say to you, rise, pick up your stretcher, and go home." [25] He stood up immediately before them, picked up what he had been lying on, and went home, glorifying God. [26] Then astonishment seized them all and they glorified God, and, struck with awe, they said, "We have seen incredible things today."

Meditation

Jesus offers a salvation that embraces the whole person. He didn't come just to save souls. He is concerned with the total person, which means both the soul and the body.[5] Jesus came to redeem and restore all that is fragmented and separated in and around us, to bring everything back into the wholeness that God intended from the beginning. As I've reflected on this, I have come to believe that God's healing entails the five primary areas that have been broken by original sin:[6]

1. relationship between us and God (spiritual)

2. relationship between us and others (relational)

3. integration within us: soul and spirit (psychological)

4. integration within us: body and soul (physical)

5. relationship between us and nature (ecological)

Can you think of any infirmity, disease, or psychological malady that is not rooted in one or more of these five primary relationships that define our lives? And yet they are not really five separate areas; they are intimately interconnected and part of a larger whole. The problem with our modern world, and especially with our scientific approaches to healing, is that we see them all separately.

In this gospel story of the paralyzed man, Jesus saw him as a whole person and healed him body, soul, and spirit. I experienced something similar to this in my experience praying for a young girl in Brazil. Like in the gospel passage, where the paralyzed man's friends brought him to Jesus, I was brought to pray for a young girl by her friends. As with the gospel story, forgiveness (from the heart) played a major role in her physical and emotional healing.

Sometimes these deadly sins remain hidden in our lives, manifesting in the most unusual ways. Such was the case with Ana, a sweet, teenage girl whom I prayed with on my final night in Brazil, along with her friends and family. Looking at Ana, you would never guess that the deadly sin of anger was crippling her—literally and figuratively.

I discovered, through my interpreter, that Ana's right hip and foot had been injured from a car accident when she was six years old. Due to the injury to her hip, Ana's right leg was about eight inches shorter than her left.

When I asked Ana if she had forgiven the man who hit her with the car, tears streamed down her cheeks. She shook her head and then spoke some words in Portuguese that I did not understand. The interpreter simply translated: "She said no, she can't forgive him, because it would hurt too much."

I was amazed at this young girl's insight, recognizing that she was holding on to bitterness to protect her from suffering her deeper pain. With that confirmation, I grew even more hopeful that we would see a miraculous healing.

As soon as Ana pronounced the words of forgiveness, I felt her leg release the full eight inches in my hand, reaching normal length. We were all amazed and began spontaneously praising Jesus for healing her. Ana was especially relieved and amazed, realizing her emotional pain had also been released. Ana's physical wound was obvious, but her deeper emotional wounds were not—neither was her "sin." The more I reflect on this experience, the more I think of the paralyzed man and why Jesus dealt with his spiritual healing first. The people could only see the externals. But Jesus saw his heart. Similarly, though the rest of us were unable to see the connections between Ana's physical, emotional, and spiritual healing, Jesus knew exactly what she needed in order to receive his powerful healing love. All we could do was offer Jesus our praise.

Vocal Prayer

Think of any time in your life where you have been healed, physically, emotionally, or spiritually. Offer praise to God from your heart in vocal prayer.

Praise Jesus for his love and any ways he has healed you. Begin by praying aloud Psalm 146:1–2. Then continue with your own words of praise:

¹ Hallelujah!
² Praise the LORD, my soul;
    I will praise the LORD all my life,
      sing praise to my God while I live.

As you praise God, anticipate the healing you will receive in the following contemplative prayer experience.

Contemplation

As you pray contemplatively with this scripture passage, ask the Holy Spirit to show you an area of paralysis in your life (physically, emotionally, or spiritually) that needs healing. Allow the Holy Spirit to guide you as you encounter Jesus in this prayer experience.

Imagine you are the paralyzed man, and your friends are bringing you to Jesus. When Jesus speaks to the paralyzed man in the story, allow his words to be directed to you *personally. For example, receive these words from Jesus as they are spoken to you: "As for **you, your** sins are forgiven. . . . I say to **you**, rise, pick up your stretcher, and go home."*

Assume a comfortable position and take a few deep breaths. Pray, "Come, Holy Spirit."

As you begin this prayer experience, call to mind any area where you feel "paralyzed." Ask the Holy Spirit to reveal this to you. It can be a physical, emotional, or spiritual paralysis. For example, trauma often freezes us, leaving us feeling paralyzed in a particular area of our life.

Imagine you are the paralyzed man brought in on a stretcher. Experience what it is like to be totally dependent upon others to bring you to Jesus.

Who are friends in your life who would go to this much trouble to bring you to Jesus for healing? Envision them carrying your stretcher and making their way up to and through the roof.

What does it feel like as you feel the push and noise of the crowd and are lifted by your friends and then brought down through the roof? Describe your experience.

What do you experience as you are brought into Jesus's presence?

How does he look at you before he speaks to you?

In what area of your life do you need to receive his forgiveness?

Take in these words: "As for you, your sins are forgiven."

What areas of spiritual or emotional paralysis in your life are healed by these words from Jesus?

Is there anyone you need to forgive (including yourself)?

Are you willing to bring these areas to Jesus in Confession?

In what ways are you feeling powerless and unable to engage in normal life?

What do you experience as you receive these words from Jesus: "I say to you, rise, pick up your stretcher, and go home"?

In what area of your personal paralysis is Jesus commanding you to rise and walk? What does that mean to you practically?

Allow some time to bask in the healing that Jesus is offering you.

What action is the Holy Spirit inspiring in you following this encounter with Jesus?

Action

Respond to your contemplative prayer experience with an action. Ask the Holy Spirit to inspire you.

Suggested Action: Pray for someone you know who is struggling with a physical ailment. As you pray, ask Jesus to heal them spiritually, emotionally, and physically. Ask the Holy Spirit to reveal any specific ways to pray for this person. Then ask him how you could be a good friend to this person (like the friends of the paralyzed man). As this is revealed, act on it.

Alternative Action: If the suggested action does not fit you, ask the Holy Spirit to inspire an action that does.

WISDOM FROM THE CHURCH

As you reflect on Day 6, allow the wisdom from the Church to help you strengthen the graces of this day.

Jesus saw the paralyzed man's physical, emotional, and spiritual ailments not as separate issues to be treated but as an interrelated whole. Like Jesus, the Church sees us in wholeness: "The unity of soul and body is so profound that one has to consider the soul to be the 'form' of the body . . . ; spirit and matter, in man, are not two natures united, but rather their union forms a single nature" (*CCC*, 365). Likewise, Pope Benedict XVI urges us to have a "whole-person perspective" as we approach Jesus in areas where we desire to be healed: "Whoever wishes to heal man must see him in his wholeness and must know that his ultimate healing can only be God's love."[7]

Jesus forgave the man in this gospel passage before he healed him physically. Forgiveness is often the key to our physical, emotional, and spiritual healing: "Now—and this is daunting—this outpouring of mercy cannot penetrate our hearts a long as we have not forgiven those who have trespassed against us. Love, like the Body of Christ, is indivisible. . . . In refusing to forgive our brothers and sisters, our hearts are closed and their hardness makes them impervious to the Father's merciful love; but in confessing our sins, our hearts are opened to grace" (*CCC*, 2840). In the Our Father, we ask to be forgiven as we too forgive others; through this forgiveness we open ourselves to God's healing love.

FURTHER GROWTH

If you desire to explore this gospel passage and the theme in more depth, here are a few suggestions for further growth.

1. Read chapters 5 and 6 of *Be Healed* (Ave Maria Press, 2014).

2. Watch a dramatization of this gospel scene in the video "Jesus Heals the Paralytic" in the YouTube series *The Chosen* (season 1, episode 6) (*The Chosen*, 2019).

3. Read *Loved as I Am* by Sr. Miriam James Heidland, SOLT (Ave Maria Press, 2014).

4. Listen to the song "Rescue" by Lauren Daigle (2018).

5. Read *Forgiveness and Inner Healing* by Betty Tapscott and Fr. Robert DeGrandis (St. Joseph's Books, 1980).

DAY 7

"HAS NO ONE CONDEMNED YOU?"

Embracing God's Mercy: Jesus and the Adulterous Woman

John 8:2–12
(Based on Chapter 7 of *Be Healed*)

PREPARATION

Place yourself in the presence of God.

This gospel account of Jesus and the woman caught in adultery shows us that none of us have the right to condemn ourselves or anyone else, because Jesus does not condemn us. God desires to heal our wounds. He wants to reach the deepest recesses of our shame and penetrate it with his merciful love. In this moving story from the Gospel of John we see that "shame is . . . swallowed up by love, dissolved in it."[8]

▌ LECTIO DIVINA
Gospel of John (8:2–12): Jesus Encounters the Woman Caught in Adultery

Take a few deep breaths. As you breathe, ask Jesus to meet you in the areas of your shame as you pray with this scripture passage.

Reading

As you read through the story the first time, pay attention to how the woman's accusers treat her when her sin is exposed. Then pay attention to how Jesus speaks to them and how he treats the woman. Finally, notice how Jesus calls her to holiness.

[2] Early in the morning [Jesus] arrived again in the temple area, and all the people started coming to him, and he sat down and taught them. [3] Then the scribes and the Pharisees brought a woman who had been caught in adultery and made her stand in the middle. [4] They said to him, "Teacher, this woman was caught in the very act of committing adultery. [5] Now in the law, Moses commanded us to stone such women. So what do you say?" [6] They said this to test him, so that they could have some charge to bring against him. Jesus

bent down and began to write on the ground with his finger. [7] But when they continued asking him, he straightened up and said to them, "Let the one among you who is without sin be the first to throw a stone at her." [8] Again he bent down and wrote on the ground. [9] And in response, they went away one by one, beginning with the elders. So he was left alone with the woman before him. [10] Then Jesus straightened up and said to her, "Woman, where are they? Has no one condemned you?" [11] She replied, "No one, sir." Then Jesus said, "Neither do I condemn you. Go, [and] from now on do not sin anymore."

[12] Jesus spoke to them again, saying, "I am the light of the world. Whoever follows me will not walk in darkness, but will have the light of life."

Meditation

Jesus encounters this woman while she is being publicly humiliated. Can you imagine the intensity of her shame? All of us know the experience of shame in our lives, even if we don't acknowledge it. Shame is insidious. Because of original sin, we intuitively know we are deficient and not all that we should be. We are all sinners. We have a fear of being exposed. We instinctively feel unworthy of

God's love, or the love of anyone else. When our sins are exposed, our shame becomes heightened.

These feelings of shame are part of our common inheritance in this fallen world. We internalize shame when we are not loved well or have been on the receiving end of others mistreatment. We also internalize shame when we sin in thought, word, or deed. Shame seems to become especially heightened when our sexuality is involved. This woman is probably experiencing shame from all these sources.

Shame is one of the deadly wounds. This woman is probably experiencing all seven of the deadly wounds identified in the table below. She is being *rejected* by the crowd and *abandoned* by her supposed lover. I can only imagine her level of *fear, powerlessness, hopelessness,* and *confusion* and her depth of shame as she is being publicly humiliated for her sin.

Table 7.1 lists the seven deadly wounds and the accompanying identity beliefs associated with them. Notice that each of the seven deadly wounds has a corresponding identity belief.[9]

Seven Deadly Wounds	Associated Identity Beliefs
Abandonment	I am all alone; no one cares or understands.
Fear	I am afraid; if I trust, I will be hurt/die.
Powerlessness	I can't change it; I'm too small/weak.
Hopelessness	Things will never get better; I want to die.
Confusion	I don't understand what is happening.
Rejection	I am not loved, wanted, or desired.
Shame	I am bad, dirty, shameful, stupid, and worthless.

When we are wounded, we often internalize messages about ourselves. This in turn deeply affects our identity, the way we see ourselves. We may believe with our intellects that we are God's beloved children, but our hearts believe a different message. For example, when we are rejected, we may believe that we are not wanted, loved, or desired. When we experience shame, we may internalize the belief that we are bad, dirty, worthless, stupid, and so forth. Which of these identity lies do you think this woman experienced?

Over the years I have accompanied many people who have experienced deep shame from their sexual wounds and sin. In chapter 7 of *Be Healed*, I tell the story of a man I called John. Like the woman caught in adultery, John experienced deep shame over his sexual compulsions and sexual sins. The only difference is that he was the one throwing stones of condemnation at himself. He identified both with the woman who was humiliated and with the accusers in the story.

John's self-condemnation (I am not lovable) increased as he grew older. This became the source of paralyzing shame, which fueled his addictions. Shame and self-condemnation are powerful forces that block our capacity to give and receive love. We need someone beyond ourselves to rescue us from this debilitating cycle of sin and shame. Like the woman caught in adultery, John eventually experienced a deep healing in his life as he encountered Jesus's merciful love. He was able to drop the "stones" of his internalized accusations and experience his identity as the beloved son of the Father through a profound experience of Jesus's merciful love.

Vocal Prayer

Recall an area of your life where you have felt ashamed over a particular sin (sexual or otherwise). Come before the Father in humility and address him in vocal prayer.

Start your conversation with God by drawing on the words in Psalm 51:3–6 of King David after he was confronted by the prophet Nathan for his adultery. Cognizant of your sin, make these words your own as you pray them aloud. Then continue expressing anything else you want to say to God.

> [3] Have mercy on me, God, in accord with your merciful love;
>> in your abundant compassion blot out my transgressions.
> [4] Thoroughly wash away my guilt;
>> and from my sin cleanse me.
> [5] For I know my transgressions;
>> my sin is always before me.
> [6] Against you, you alone have I sinned;
>> I have done what is evil in your eyes

So that you are just in your word,
    and without reproach in your judgment.

You can experience your own personal encounter with Jesus's mercy through the following contemplative prayer activity.

Contemplation

As you pray contemplatively with this scripture passage describing Jesus's encounter with the woman caught in adultery, ask the Holy Spirit to show you an area of sexual sin and shame in your past or present. Allow the Holy Spirit to guide your imagination as you encounter Jesus in this prayer experience.

*Imagine yourself in the place of the woman caught in adultery. When Jesus speaks to the accusers and the woman in the story, allow his words to be directed to you personally. For example, receive these words from Jesus directed to you: "Has no one condemned **you**? . . . Neither do I condemn **you**."*

Ask the Holy Spirit to highlight an area of sin and shame in your life (past or present).

Imagine yourself being publicly exposed while your sin is broadcast through the streets of your neighborhood or at church. What are you feeling as this is taking place?

Who are your accusers? (They could include yourself, the "father of lies," or others who have condemned you.)

What do you believe about yourself as they accuse you? What are the words of condemnation you hear in your mind? Write them down to bring them into the light. How do you feel when you hear these accusations?

What are you experiencing as Jesus writes on the ground and speaks these words to your accusers: "Let the one among you who is without sin be the first to throw a stone"?

After your accusers disappear, Jesus is now looking at you and speaking these words: "Has no one condemned you? Neither do I condemn you. Go, and from now on do not sin anymore." (Spend as much time as you need experiencing this encounter in your imagination.)

What are you experiencing as Jesus speaks these words to you? What do you desire to say to him?

Jesus then speaks these words of encouragement to you. "I am the light of the world. Follow me and you will not walk in darkness but will have the light of life."

What are your thoughts, feelings, and desires? Write these down in your prayer journal.

What action proceeds from this prayer experience?

Action

Respond to your contemplative prayer experience with an action. Ask the Holy Spirit to inspire you.

Suggested Action: Identify a person you have been judging, accusing, and condemning either with your words or in your thoughts. (That person could be yourself, God, another person in your life now, someone from your past, a public figure, or someone else.) Write out the judgments that you have been holding against this person. Ask God's forgiveness for your judgments and for that person. Then renounce, one by one, these condemning accusations. For example, "In the name of Jesus Christ, I renounce the accusation that (insert person's name and identify the condemning judgments or accusations)." Do that for each of your condemning judgements and accusations. Then ask Jesus to reveal his mercy to this person. And in place of each judgment, bless this person, affirming their true identity as a beloved child of God.

Alternative Action: If the suggested action does not fit you, ask the Holy Spirit to inspire an action that does.

WISDOM FROM THE CHURCH

As you reflect on Day 7, allow the wisdom from the Church to help you strengthen the graces of this day.

St. John Paul II writes in his *Theology of the Body* about the impact of shame in our lives: "Shame touches . . . the deepest level and seems to shake the very foundation of [our] existence. A certain fear is always a part of the very essence of shame."[10]

The Church shows us how we can transform this shame and condemnation into compassion: "It is there, in fact, 'in the depths of the *heart*,' that everything is bound and loosed. It is not in our power not to feel or to forget an offense; but the heart that offers itself to the Holy Spirit turns injury into compassion and purifies the memory in transforming the hurt into intercession" (*CCC*, 2843). Through our own experiences of sin and shame and of healing and grace, we can learn empathy and compassion toward others.

Allowing Jesus's merciful love to penetrate our shame allows us to move out of self-condemnation. Our integrity is restored as we overcome sin and learn to love chastely: "The chaste person maintains the integrity of the powers of life and love placed in him. This integrity ensures the unity of the person; it is opposed to any behavior that would impair it" (*CCC*, 2338). Chastity is a call to love completely.

FURTHER GROWTH

If you desire to explore this gospel passage and the theme in more depth, here are a few suggestions for further growth.

1. Read chapter 7 of *Be Healed* (Ave Maria Press, 2014).

2. Watch the video *The Heart of Man*, directed by Eric Esau (documentary about the Father's mercy for those struggling with sexual sin, compulsion, and shame) (Sypher Studios, 2017).

3. Read *The Soul of Shame* by Curt Thompson (Inter-Varsity Press, 2015).

4. Listen to the song "Out of Hiding" by Steffany Gretzinger (2014).

5. Read *Be Restored: Healing our Sexual Wounds through Jesus' Merciful Love* by Bob Schuchts (Ave Maria Press, 2021).

"CAN YOU DRINK THE CUP?"

Redeeming Our Suffering: Jesus and His Disciples (Part 1)

Mark 10:35–45
(Based on Chapter 8 of *Be Healed*)

PREPARATION

Place yourself in the presence of God.

This story of Jesus with his disciples, from the Gospel of Mark, highlights Jesus's redemptive suffering borne out of his humility and self-giving love. This is contrasted by his disciples' self-seeking, borne out of their pride and selfishness. We are encouraged to ask ourselves: Are we more like Jesus or his disciples in our response to suffering? Jesus asks each of us, as he asks his disciples: "Can you drink the cup (of my suffering)"?

According to St. John Paul II in his apostolic letter *Salvifici Dolores (On Human Suffering)* every man is called to "drink the cup" with Jesus: "The Redeemer suffered in place of man and for man. Every man has his own share in the redemption. Each one is called to share in that suffering through which the redemption is accomplished. . . . Thus each man, in his suffering, can also become a sharer in the redemptive suffering of Christ" (19).

LECTIO DIVINA
Gospel of Mark (10:32–45): Jesus Invites His Disciples to Share in His Redemptive Suffering

Take a few deep breaths. As you breathe, invite the Holy Spirit to inspire you as you pray with this scripture passage.

Reading
As you read through the gospel passage, pay attention to Jesus's interactions with his disciples. Listen to what Jesus tells them about his impending suffering, death, and resurrection. Notice how his disciples respond: by focusing on themselves, motivated by pride and envy. What does Jesus ask of them?

32 They were on the way, going up to Jerusalem, and Jesus went ahead of them. They were amazed, and those who followed were afraid. Taking the Twelve aside again, he began to tell them what was going to happen to him. 33 "Behold, we are going up to Jerusalem, and the Son of Man will be handed over to the chief priests and the scribes, and they will condemn him to death and hand him over to the Gentiles 34 who will mock him, spit upon him, scourge him, and put him to death, but after three days he will rise."

35 Then James and John, the sons of Zebedee, came to him and said to him, "Teacher, we want you to do for us whatever we ask of you." 36 He replied, "What do you wish [me] to do for you?" 37 They answered him, "Grant that in your glory we may sit one at your right and the other at your left." 38 Jesus said to them, "You do not know what you are asking. Can you drink the cup that I drink or be baptized with the baptism with which I am baptized?" 39 They said to him, "We can." Jesus said to them, "The cup that I drink, you will drink, and with the baptism with which I am baptized, you will be baptized; 40 but to sit at my right or at my left is not mine to give but is for those for whom it has been prepared." 41 When the ten heard this, they

became indignant at James and John. ⁴²Jesus summoned them and said to them, "You know that those who are recognized as rulers over the Gentiles lord it over them, and their great ones make their authority over them felt. ⁴³But it shall not be so among you. Rather, whoever wishes to be great among you will be your servant; ⁴⁴whoever wishes to be first among you will be the slave of all. ⁴⁵For the Son of Man did not come to be served but to serve and to give his life as a ransom for many."

Meditation

Several years ago, during Holy Week, I went with members of our parish community to see the movie *The Passion of the Christ*. I knew it would not be easy to watch, but it ended up being harder than I imagined, especially during the scene of Jesus's scourging. I wanted to turn away as I saw Jesus brutalized by the soldier's repeated lashings. With each crushing blow, as more blood oozed from his torn flesh, I numbed myself all the more. I could understand with new depth the words of Psalm 38: "I am numb and utterly crushed; I wail with anguish of heart" (Ps 38:9). In the Garden of Gethsemane Jesus wailed as his heart was filled with anguish (see Matthew 26:36–38), but here at the pillar he was simply numb and utterly crushed. His mother Mary, his followers, and all the other onlookers were similarly traumatized—as were many of us who watched the reenactment.

Whether as observers or participants, we all know soul-numbing trauma in our lives: death's anguish, the tearing apart of hearts and families through divorce, the violence of abuse; the list goes on. Suffering is all around us and has touched each of our lives personally, in one way or another. All we need to do is turn on the evening news, and it is right before our eyes. And every single day we wake up in the morning to carry our own crosses, big or small. Yet in the midst of it, we are encouraged to carry these crosses with joy and not sadness.[11] How is this possible? If you are anything like me, your instinct is to run from suffering and turn away from all the overwhelming pain that surrounds it. We all have a healthy repugnance for every form of evil and the suffering that accompanies it. This is natural. Our first and most natural response is to avoid it at any cost.

When we speak of redemptive suffering, we are not suggesting that suffering itself is good. As Pope John Paul II affirms in his apostolic letter *Salvifici Dolores (On Human Suffering)*, suffering is an experience of evil. There is nothing glamorous about evil or its effects, and the Cross makes this perfectly clear for all to see. Even Jesus prayed that his cup of suffering would be taken away from him, before surrendering to his Father's will for our sakes (Mt 26:3). He knew that he was about to enter into the most difficult battle with evil that any human being could ever face. And yet he did it willingly, because he knew that his suffering would redeem the world.

If the Passion story were to end with the Crucifixion, we would have no choice but to resign ourselves to the inevitable despair of spending our lives in misery. This would be hell on earth. But the Gospel story does not end in meaningless suffering and despair. Jesus didn't remain stuck on the Cross or in death; he triumphed in the Resurrection. Because of Christ's victory over sin and death, the Cross has become the font of our healing and redemption.

Jesus invites all his disciples, including us, to receive the grace of his redemption and to share in his redemptive suffering. When offered in humility and self-giving love, in communion with Jesus, our daily sufferings will bring healing to us personally and to all those around us.

Vocal Prayer

Think of any area of your life where you have experienced suffering. Offer this suffering to the Father in union with Jesus, in vocal prayer.

Start by praying aloud these words from Psalm 38:9–10, 16. Then continue offering your suffering to the Father with Jesus and ask for his redemption.

> ⁹ I am numb and utterly crushed;
>> I wail with anguish of heart
> ¹⁰ My Lord, my deepest yearning is before you;
>> my groaning is not hidden from you.
> ¹⁶ LORD, it is for you that I wait;
>> O Lord, my God, you respond.

In the following contemplative prayer experience I encourage you to join your personal suffering with Jesus's, so that it can be a source of healing for yourself and many others.

Contemplation

As you pray contemplatively with this gospel account of Jesus interacting with his disciples, imagine yourself as the disciple John. Remember he ended up at the foot of the Cross with the Blessed Mother, Mary Magdalene, and others.

*When Jesus speaks to John (and James), allow his words to be directed to you personally. For example, receive these words from Jesus directed to you: "Can **you** drink the cup that I drink or be baptized with the baptism with which I am baptized?"*

To make this more personal, ask the Holy Spirit to show you a time (past or present) when you responded selfishly to another's suffering.

Imagine that this suffering person is Jesus (see Acts 9 and Matthew 25 to see how Jesus is totally united with each person in their suffering).

With that context, engage your heart in this prayer experience.

Jesus describes to you the horrible suffering that he is going to experience. What are you experiencing as he tells you about this?

You respond as John did (see Mark 10:35, 37) by ignoring Jesus words and asking instead for a position of glory. What is going on inside you?

When the other disciples become indignant with you, how do you feel?

Jesus then asks you directly, "Can you drink the cup that I drink?"

What are you experiencing as Jesus speaks these words to you? What do you desire to say to him?

Jesus then shows you how to be great in his kingdom, by being a servant of the rest. How do you respond?

Now jump ahead to the Passion of Christ. (You may want to contemplate the Passion with the gospel account, with the Sorrowful Mysteries of the Rosary, or with the Stations of the Cross.)

All of these events that Jesus predicted now unfold before your eyes.

You watch Jesus as he is handed over to the chief priests and the scribes, and then condemned to death. What are you experiencing?

You are close by as you see the Roman soldiers mock him, spit upon him, and then scourge him. What is going through your mind? What are you feeling? What do you desire?

You watch them nail his hands and feet and put the cross in the ground. You are present for every agonizing moment. You remember your reaction when he told you this was going to happen. How are you feeling in this moment?

His mother, Mary, and Mary of Magdalene stand by your side at the foot of the cross. Jesus looks directly upon you in the midst of his suffering and says, "Behold your mother." What are you experiencing?

Three days later you hear reports from Mary Magdalene that the tomb is empty. You and Peter run to the tomb and find his linen cloths folded up. What is going through your mind? What are you feeling?

Summarize your thoughts, feelings, and desires from this contemplative prayer experience.

What action are you being called to?

Action

Respond to your contemplative prayer experience with an action. Ask the Holy Spirit to inspire you.

Suggested Action: Identify an area of your personal suffering. Ask the Father to show you how can you unite this suffering with Jesus as a way of participating in his redemptive love. Then find a tangible way to comfort another person in their suffering this week, showing them Jesus's love and compassion.

Alternative Action: If the suggested action does not fit you, ask the Holy Spirit to inspire an action that does.

WISDOM FROM THE CHURCH

As you reflect on Day 8, allow the wisdom from the Church to help you strengthen the graces of this day.

St. John Paul II addresses the dangers of seeking positions of power like James and John: "In Christ no one is inferior and no one is superior. All are *members of the same body,* seeking one another's happiness and wishing to build a world which embraces everyone. . . . Brotherhood rejects the desire for power, and service the temptation of power" ("Meditation for 12th World Youth Day," 4).

The *Catechism* shows instead that real power lies in redemptive suffering: "It is love 'to the end' that confers on Christ's sacrifice its value as redemption and reparation. . . . He knew and loved us all when he offered his life" (*CCC*, 616). "'The possibility of being made partners, in a way known to God, in the paschal mystery' is offered to all men" (*CCC*, 618).

Jesus models for us how to suffer redemptively by surrendering his will to the Father's will, St. John Paul reflects in *Rosarium Virginis Mariae* (*On the Most Holy Rosary*): "The Gospels give great prominence to the sorrowful mysteries of Christ. The sequence of meditations begins with Gethsemane. . . . There Jesus encounters all the temptations and confronts all the sins of humanity, in order to say to the Father: 'Not my will but yours be done' (Lk 22:42 and parallels)" (22). When we follow

Jesus's example and see our sufferings as an opportunity to love, we participate in his salvific healing mission.

FURTHER GROWTH

If you desire to explore this gospel passage and the theme in more depth, here are a few suggestions for further growth.

1.   Read chapter 8 of *Be Healed* (Ave Maria Press, 2014).

2.   Watch the movie *The Passion of the Christ*, directed by Mel Gibson (Icon, 2004).

3.   Read *Salvifici Doloris: On the Christian Meaning of Human Suffering* by Pope John Paul II (St. Paul Editions, 1984).

4.   Listen to the song "More Like Jesus" by Passion Music (2018).

5.   Read *Real Suffering: Finding Hope & Healing in the Trials of Life* by Bob Schuchts (St. Benedict Press, 2018).

DAY 9

"HAVE YOU COME TO BELIEVE?"

Unleashing the Sacraments:
Jesus and His Disciples (Part 2)

John 20:19–29
(Based on Chapter 9 of *Be Healed*)

PREPARATION

Place yourself in the presence of God.

This gospel account, witnessed and written by the apostle John, describes Jesus appearing to his disciples after the Resurrection. It represents a crucial moment in the sacramental life of the Church. As the disciples receive the Holy Spirit from the risen Jesus, they are given the grace to bring his healing love to many through the sacraments. But first they must believe in what they see, so that we can believe in what we can't see through these sacramental signs. Our firm belief is rooted in the knowledge that Jesus gave his Spirit and authority to the apostles: "Thus the risen Christ, by giving the Holy Spirit to the apostles, entrusted to them his power of sanctifying: they became sacramental signs of Christ" (*CCC*, 1087).

LECTIO DIVINA
Gospel of John (20:19–29): Jesus Appears to His Disciples after His Resurrection

Take a few deep breaths. As you breathe, invite the Holy Spirit to inspire you as you pray with this scripture passage.

Reading

As you read through the gospel story, pay attention to Jesus's interactions with his disciples. Notice the words he speaks to them and the actions associated with his words. Notice how his disciples respond, especially Thomas.

[19] On the evening of that first day of the week, when the doors were locked, where the disciples were, for fear of the Jews, Jesus came and stood in their midst and said to them, "Peace be with you." [20] When he had

said this, he showed them his hands and his side. The disciples rejoiced when they saw the Lord. [21] [Jesus] said to them again, "Peace be with you. As the Father has sent me, so I send you." [22] And when he had said this, he breathed on them and said to them, "Receive the holy Spirit. [23] Whose sins you forgive are forgiven them, and whose sins you retain are retained."

[24] Thomas, called Didymus, one of the Twelve, was not with them when Jesus came. [25] So the other disciples said to him, "We have seen the Lord." But he said to them, "Unless I see the mark of the nails in his hands and put my finger into the nail marks and put my hand into his side, I will not believe." [26] Now a week later his disciples were again inside and Thomas was with them. Jesus came, although the doors were locked, and stood in their midst and said, "Peace be with you." [27] Then he said to Thomas, "Put your finger here and see my hands, and bring your hand and put it into my side, and do not be unbelieving, but believe." [28] Thomas answered and said to him, "My Lord and my God!" [29] Jesus said to him, "Have you come to believe because you have seen me? Blessed are those who have not seen and have believed."

Meditation

A big part of my growth in believing what I could not
see—that is, Jesus's healing presence in the sacraments—
came from witnessing my brother Dave's transforma-
tion. The sacraments played a vital role in bringing him
back to Jesus and healing his soul. After spending more
than twenty years bound by an addiction to heroin and
in jail several times, Dave experienced a life-changing
Confession with my pastor in the Sacrament of Reconciliation. The priest, who was anointed with the Spirit
and in the apostolic succession of the disciples, operated
in Jesus's authority to forgive Dave's sins ("Whose sins
you forgive are forgiven"). A few years later, while on
his death bed, Dave was restored back to life for a short
time through the Sacrament of Anointing of the Sick.
This led to incredible healing with Dave and our family.

In between Dave's life-changing Confession and his
subsequent death, we grieved as we saw him become pro-
gressively more infirmed due to HIV (contracted from
a heroin needle). As we watched Dave declining both
physically and mentally, our family earnestly prayed for
his healing. But one night, I had a dream where I sensed
the Holy Spirit saying: *You are praying for Dave's healing, but he is going to die with this illness. Through his*

dying process your entire family will receive much healing. Knowing that Dave was close to death, my sister Margaret and I traveled the three hours to visit him and my brother Wayne. When we arrived at Wayne's home, we were distraught to find Dave in a coma. Margaret and I had both hoped to have one last chance to say goodbye to Dave before he died. Disheartened and concerned he might die at any minute, we called a local priest (whom we didn't know) to give Dave the Sacrament of Anointing of the Sick. Dave remained unconscious as the priest prayed for him, and we all participated. After thanking the priest, Wayne, Margaret, and I decided to go for a run to plan Dave's funeral. The home health worker stayed behind in another room, leaving Dave alone in the bedroom.

After we finished our run and headed into the house, we were startled by a magnificent sight: Dave was awake. He tried getting out of bed. We shouted for him to wait and ran into his bedroom. Overjoyed to see Dave awake again, we all gave him a big hug, all the while celebrating our own personal Lazarus experience (see John 11). Dave went on to tell us what happened. He said he felt himself slipping into death, but at the moment of the anointing he encountered Jesus in heaven. Jesus told him it was not yet time for him to come home and that there was something more for him to do.

Though Dave would live only another two weeks after receiving the sacrament, this resuscitation from death became a profound healing for many of us in the family and helped fulfill Dave's purpose of being someone with AIDS for Christ. That next afternoon, Dave's daughter, Sarah (then eight years old), and her mother came to say goodbye. We were all touched as we watched them interact with tender love and depart from one another while enveloped in supernatural peace.

As a result of the sacramental anointing, other family members had the opportunity to say goodbye to Dave. Over those final two weeks of Dave's life, my mom, her parents, her brother Sam, and my brother Bart all came to visit Dave. The crowning gift in the Father's providence came as Dad, Margie, and I were able to be with him in his final moments of life.

I will never again look at the Sacrament of Anointing of the Sick with indifference. I now see its two purposes clearly: (1) the restoration of health and (2) the preparation for passing over to eternal life (see *CCC*, 1532). I now realize that all the sacraments are genuine encounters with the crucified and risen Jesus. The Holy Spirit works through them powerfully when we have the faith to believe what we cannot see.

Vocal Prayer

Think of a grace you have received through the sacraments. Give thanks to God for that grace in vocal prayer.

Start your prayer by praying aloud these words from Psalm 116:4, 8, 13, 17. Then continue offering your "sacrifice of praise" to the Father by thanking him for how he has freed you from death through his sacraments.

4 Then I called on the name of the LORD,
   "O LORD, save my life!"
8 For my soul has been freed from death,
   my eyes from tears, my feet from stumbling.
13 I will raise the cup of salvation
   and call on the name of the LORD.
17 I will offer a sacrifice of praise
   and call on the name of the LORD.

As you enter into the following contemplative prayer experience, ask the Holy Spirit to give you faith to believe what you cannot see.

Contemplation

*As you pray contemplatively with this scripture passage
of Jesus appearing to his disciples in his resurrected body,
ask the Holy Spirit to bring you into a genuine encounter with the risen Jesus. The Church and scriptures teach
us that the sacraments are visible manifestations of this
invisible reality.*

*I encourage you to engage in this contemplative prayer
experience in relationship with one of the sacraments.
Receive Jesus's words from this gospel passage as they are
directed to you personally. For example, during and after
receiving Jesus's crucified and resurrected body in the Eucharist, or after being forgiven of your sins in Confession, receive
these words as they are spoken to you personally: "Peace be
with **you**."*

*Ask the Holy Spirit to lead you into a deeper encounter
with the risen Jesus through this prayer experience.*

*Ponder times when you have not believed or failed to
reverence Jesus's presence in the sacraments.*

*As you go to Confession, realize Jesus has given his power
and authority to the priest. Jesus is present in his resurrected
power to forgive your sins. When the priest speaks the words
of absolution, your sins are forgiven by the Lord himself:
"Whose sins you forgive are forgiven."*

Spend some time contemplating that reality that Jesus has forgiven you. Hear these words spoken to you personally: "Peace be with you." Allow his peace to fill you, body and soul. What do you experience?

The Eucharist is Jesus resurrected body, which you can see and touch, just as Thomas did in the upper room. Silently in your heart proclaim: "We have seen the Lord."

During the consecration at Mass, speak these words to Jesus in your heart: "My Lord and my God."

After receiving Jesus's resurrected body in the Eucharist hear again these words: "Peace be with you." Spend some time in contemplation savoring his presence and feeling the peace.

Wherever you may have doubts about Jesus's resurrected presence in the sacraments, hear these words: "Do not be unbelieving, but believe."

As you reaffirm your faith in his presence, hear Jesus say to you: "Blessed are those who have not seen and have believed."

Following this contemplative prayer experience, record your thoughts, feelings, and desires in your prayer journal.

What action are you being called to as you contemplate these mysteries?

Action

Respond to your contemplative prayer experience with an action. Ask the Holy Spirit to inspire you.

Suggested Action: Spend an hour in adoration praying for more faith for yourself or someone you know who does not believe in Jesus's living presence in the sacraments. Then share your faith with someone who may not believe as you do.

Alternative Action: If the suggested action does not fit you, ask the Holy Spirit to inspire an action that does.

WISDOM FROM THE CHURCH

As you reflect on Day 9, allow the wisdom from the Church to help you strengthen the graces of this day.

The sacraments are the work of the Holy Spirit through Christ's mystical body, the Church: "Sacraments are 'powers that comes forth' from the Body of Christ, which is ever-living and life-giving. They are actions of the Holy Spirit at work in his Body, the Church" (*CCC*, 1116). Jesus continues to offer healing through his sacraments.

The sacraments are means for us to live Christ's risen life: "The desire and work of the Spirit in the heart of the Church is that we may live from the life of the risen Christ" (*CCC*, 1091). They enable us to receive eternal life.

We are able to see and believe what remains unseen in the sacraments through contemplative prayer: "The mystery of Christ is celebrated by the Church in the Eucharist, and the Holy Spirit makes it come alive in contemplative prayer" (*CCC*, 2718). By contemplating the mysteries of the sacraments, we can grow in appreciation of these important gifts that Jesus has given us to experience his healing love.

FURTHER GROWTH

If you desire to explore this gospel passage and the theme in more depth, here are a few suggestions for further growth.

1. Read chapter 9 of *Be Healed* (Ave Maria Press, 2014).

2. Watch the video "Heaven on Earth: Have You Heard of These Eucharistic Miracles?" on YouTube (Aleteia, 2020).

3. Read *Swear to God: The Promise and Power of the Sacraments* by Scott Hahn (Image, 2004).

4. Listen to the song "Christ Is Risen" by Matt Maher (2009).

5. Read *Be Transformed: The Healing Power of the Sacraments* by Bob Schuchts (Ave Maria Press, 2017).

"DO YOU LOVE ME MORE THAN THESE?"

Resurrecting Our Mission: Jesus and Peter

John 21:1, 7, 9, 12–17
(Based on Chapter 10 of *Be Healed*)

PREPARATION

Place yourself in the presence of God.

This passage from John's gospel focuses on Peter being restored by Jesus after his threefold denial. This healing encounter between Jesus and Peter takes place in front of a charcoal fire with witnesses (perhaps reminding Peter of his denial in front of a charcoal fire in front of witnesses). Jesus heals this memory by asking Peter three times to reaffirm his love and faith. Thus, Jesus heals Peter's wounds and restores his mission and identity.

Each one of us needs a similar healing and restoration: The human heart is heavy and hardened; God must give each of us a new heart (see Ezekiel 36:26–27). "Conversion is first of all a work of the grace of God who makes our hearts return to him: 'Restore us to thyself, O LORD, that we may be restored!' [Lam 5:21]" (*CCC*, 1432).

LECTIO DIVINA
Gospel of John (21:1, 7, 9, 12–17): Jesus Restores Simon Peter

Take a few deep breaths. As you breathe, invite the Holy Spirit to inspire you as you pray with this scripture passage.

Reading
As you read through the gospel story, pay attention to the love, forgiveness, and trust Jesus shows to Peter as he restores their relationship. How does Peter respond? Notice how his response leads to a strong commitment of love and how he is in turn asked to serve others.

[1] After this, Jesus revealed himself again to his disciples at the Sea of Tiberias. [7] When Simon Peter heard that it was the Lord, he tucked in his garment, for he was lightly clad, and jumped into the sea. [9] When they

climbed out on shore, they saw a charcoal fire with fish on it and bread. ¹² Jesus said to them, "Come, have breakfast." And none of the disciples dared to ask him, "Who are you?" because they realized it was the Lord. ¹³ Jesus came over and took the bread and gave it to them, and in like manner the fish. ¹⁴ This was now the third time Jesus was revealed to his disciples after being raised from the dead.

¹⁵ When they had finished breakfast, Jesus said to Simon Peter, "Simon, son of John, do you love me more than these?" He said to him, "Yes, Lord, you know that I love you." He said to him, "Feed my lambs." ¹⁶ He then said to him a second time, "Simon, son of John, do you love me?" He said to him, "Yes, Lord, you know that I love you." He said to him, "Tend my sheep." ¹⁷ He said to him the third time, "Simon, son of John, do you love me?" Peter was distressed that he had said to him a third time, "Do you love me?" and he said to him, "Lord, you know everything; you know that I love you." [Jesus] said to him, "Feed my sheep."

Meditation

As he did with Simon Peter, Jesus often brings us back to our memories where we have unhealed wounds and unconfessed sins that have kept us bound (strongholds).

He does this in order to heal us and restore our freedom. Once healed and liberated, we are then able to receive our identity as beloved sons or daughters and live more fully in our God given mission.

Freedom is a great gift. The desire for it is written deeply within each of our hearts. And yet, we often exercise our liberty in ways that do not bring about our true and lasting good. As a result, we are left imprisoned, bound up in shame and hiding behind walls of fear and self-protection. We remain driven by our wounds and compulsions and become slaves of sin.

Freedom for its own sake is wonderful but not enough. We must learn how "to use it consciously for everything that is our true good," St. John Paul II writes in *Redemptor Hominis (Redeemer of Man)* (21)." Being set free from strongholds (the seven deadly sins and seven deadly wounds) is a great freedom, but it cannot be our ultimate goal. We must exercise our newfound freedom for the good of everyone around us and ultimately for the glory of God.

This glorious liberty allows us to see others and know who they are and what they need. We become capable of pursuing the good of those around us and in the process discover the greatest possible good for ourselves: our own dignity and purpose.

Do you want to be healed? Is there any area of your life that you believe disqualifies you from receiving God's grace and healing? If so, your God is not big enough, and Jesus's Cross is not real enough. In one of my favorite passages of scripture, we are given this amazing promise from God: Instead of your shame you will have a double portion of honor (see Isaiah 61:7). Think of the most shameful or hopeless area of your life, past or present. That is the place you most need a Savior to set you free. That same area in your life, when it is healed, will bring God the greatest glory in your life. For many of you, this will be the place that God will equip you to administer healing to others.

Peter is a great example of being restored in this way. Once liberated, he was able to use his freedom for good—Jesus turned his shame into glory and called him to live for others.

Vocal Prayer

Think of any area of your life where you have experienced freedom and restoration. Give thanks and praise to God in vocal prayer.

Start your prayer by praying aloud these words from Psalm 103:1–5. Then continue with your own words of thanks and praise.

¹ Bless the LORD, my soul;
  all my being bless his holy name!
² Bless the LORD, my soul;
  do not forget all his gifts,
³ Who pardons all your sins,
  and heals all your ills,
⁴ Who redeems your life from the pit,
  and crowns you with mercy and compassion,
⁵ Who fills your days with good things,
  so your youth is renewed like the eagle's.

Continue speaking out the things the Lord has done for you in this scriptural retreat.

As you enter into the following contemplative prayer experience, I invite you to think about how the Lord has restored you, and any areas that still need to be restored. What is your identity before the Father? What is the mission that the Lord is calling you to live out?

Contemplation

As you pray contemplatively with this scripture passage describing Jesus's interaction with Peter on the seashore, ask the Holy Spirit to bring you into a genuine encounter with the risen Jesus.

*Allow Jesus's words to Peter in this passage to speak to you personally. For example, "(Insert your name), do **you** love me more than these? . . . Feed my lambs."*

Begin this prayer experience by consciously placing yourself in communion with the Trinity.

Ask the Holy Spirit to remind you of an encounter with Jesus in your life where he affirmed your identity and calling.

As you immerse yourself in this memory, be attentive to how you think and what you feel. (Spend some time basking in the memory.)

Then ask the Holy Spirit to show you an area of your life where you have experienced restoration, or where you need to be restored. It may be a past memory or a present situation. It could be an area of your own sin (which is a form of denial of Jesus) or an area where you were hurt in some way.

As you recall this memory or current situation, pay attention to what you think, feel, and desire.

Now envision yourself in the presence of Jesus. He first reminds you of that moment of encounter when he affirmed your identity and mission. Then he brings you back to the more painful memory. Use your senses to immerse yourself in this memory.

In light of these memories, he asks you: "Do you love me more than these?" How do you respond?

He then tells you, "Feed my lambs." What does this mean to you?

He speaks to you a second time, using your full name, asking, "Do you love me?" How do you respond?

He then tells you, "Tend my sheep."

He asks you a third time, speaking your name: "Do you love me?" What are you feeling? How do you respond?

He then tells you, "Feed my sheep."

What mission has he entrusted to you personally?

In what way do you feel called to feed and tend his lambs and sheep?

What do you experience in this encounter with Jesus? Write down your thoughts, feelings, and desires in your prayer journal.

What action are you being called to following this time of contemplation?

Action

Respond to your contemplative prayer experience with an action. Ask the Holy Spirit to inspire you.

Suggested Action: Step out in faith to put your unique mission into action. Think of a tangible step that you can take to tend Jesus's lambs and feed his sheep in a way that fits with the desires and calling that he has placed in your heart.

Alternative Action: If the suggested action does not fit you, ask the Holy Spirit to inspire an action that does.

WISDOM FROM THE CHURCH

As you reflect on Day 10, allow the wisdom from the Church to help you strengthen the graces of this day.

Jesus asked Peter if he loved him with the highest love (charity). The Church teaches that this love is central to every mission: "Charity is the theological virtue by which we love God above all things for his own sake, and our neighbor as ourselves for the love of God" (*CCC*, 1822).

We are unable to love like this on our own. We need to grow in this virtue through prayer: "Christian prayer tries above all to meditate on the mysteries of Christ. . . . This form of prayerful reflection is of great value, but Christian prayer should go further: to the knowledge of the love of the Lord Jesus, to union with him" (*CCC*, 2708). Through frequent meditation on scripture, we can grow in knowing, loving, and becoming like Jesus, following his example more closely.

Like St. Peter, and the other apostles, we are all called to feed Jesus's lambs and tend his sheep. St. John Paul II writes in *Redemptoris Missio (Mission of the Redeemer)*: "In the apostles, the Church received a universal mission—one which knows no boundaries. . . . The Church was sent by Christ to reveal and communicate the love of God to all people and nations" (31). We are all called to share our love for Jesus in mission to others.

FURTHER GROWTH

If you desire to explore this gospel passage and the theme in more depth, here are a few suggestions for further growth.

1. Read chapter 10 and the conclusion of *Be Healed* (Ave Maria Press, 2014).

2. Watch a dramatization of "Jesus Calls Peter" in the YouTube series *The Chosen* (season 1, episode 4) (*The Chosen*, 2020).

3. Read *Fruitful Discipleship* by Sherry A. Weddell (Our Sunday Visitor, 2017).

4. Listen to the song "Jesus We Love You" by Paul McClure (2014).

5. Read *Undone* (for women) by Carrie Schuchts Daunt (Ave Maria Press, 2020) or *Man Your Post* (for men) by Duane and Carrie Daunt (TAN, 2021).

CONCLUSION

Encountering Jesus changes us forever. The more time we spend with him, St. Paul says, the more we become like him. "All of us, gazing with unveiled face on the glory of the Lord, are being transformed into the same image from glory to glory, as from the Lord who is the Spirit" (2 Cor 3:18).

Can you perceive changes in yourself as a result of encountering Jesus through prayer and contemplation during this scriptural retreat? I encourage you to explore this question in your prayer journal as a way of summarizing your overall experience. Take your time reflecting on the following questions and write down your answers. Then, a month from now, come back to reflect on what you have written, to see how your growth is continuing. Wherever you see growth and healing, spend time thanking and praising Jesus for what he has done. This will increase the graces you have received.

- After going through this retreat, is there a difference in the way you read and pray with scripture? Describe what is different.

- Has your love and desire for Jesus increased? How is this manifested in your daily life?

- Have you experienced healing in any of your (past or present) relationships? Describe the specific healing and its fruit in your life.

- Do you have more hope and trust in Jesus's desire and ability to heal you? What difference has this made in the way you approach your physical, emotional, and spiritual afflictions.

- What area of your life (physically, emotionally, or spiritually) has Jesus healed during this time? How did that healing experience take place? Be specific.

- Have you become more attracted to Jesus and spiritual riches and less attached to worldly goods? What have you renounced and what have you received?

- How have your beliefs about Jesus, yourself, and other people been transformed?

- How has your understanding and experience of the Father changed?

- Do you notice a greater freedom from shame and self-condemnation in any area of your life? Describe how you see yourself differently in those areas.

- Do you perceive and respond to the needs of others with more compassion? How is this compassion revealed in your actions?

- Do you experience more grace and hope in the areas where you have experienced suffering, past or present?

- How has your perception and reception of the sacraments changed? Are you more open to the Holy Spirit? Has your faith increased?

- Do you have any clearer understanding of your identity and personal mission? How does Jesus see you? How is he calling you to "tend his sheep?"

In whatever way you still feel stuck and discouraged, continue to pour out your heart to him, in lament and petition. You can continue growing spiritually and experiencing Jesus's ongoing healing in every area of your life. The resources mentioned at the end of each day of the retreat are offered to further your growth and healing, so consider going back to the chapter(s) that touched you most (or where you struggled the most) and explore with the additional resources. You may also find helpful resources on our website at jpiihealingcenter.org. Most importantly, dedicate yourself to daily prayer and to praying through the gospel stories with lectio divina, on a regular basis.

Finally, if you went through this retreat on your own, consider inviting a few people from your family or community to go through it together with you. Your healing will bring healing to others, simply by the way you love them. And your testimony will give them hope for what Jesus desires to do for them. Like the Samaritan woman, go and tell everyone what Jesus has done in your life.

NOTES

1. Pope John Paul II, *Man and Woman He Created Them: A Theology of the Body*, trans. Michael Waldstein (Boston: Pauline Books and Media, 2006), 28:5.

2. Pope Francis, "Homily on the Beatitudes during Daily Mass," June 10, 2013.

3. See Jack Frost, *Spiritual Slavery to Spiritual Sonship* (Shippensburg, PA: Destiny Image, 2006).

4. Henri Nouwen, *Return of the Prodigal Son: A Meditation on Fathers, Brothers, and Sons.* (London: Darton, Longman and Todd, 1992).

5. Fr. Emiliano Tardif, *Jesus Lives Today!* (South Bend, IN: Greenlawn Press, 1990), 55–56.

6. International Catholic Charismatic Renewal Services (ICCRS) Doctrinal Commission, *Guidelines for Prayers for Healing*, 5th ed. (Vatican City: ICCRS, 2017), 37–39.

7. Pope Benedict XVI, *Jesus of Nazareth: From the Baptism in the Jordan to the Transfiguration* (New York: Doubleday, 2007), 177.

8. Karol Wojtyła, *Love and Responsibility* (San Francisco: Ignatius Press, 1993), 181.

9. This list of seven wounds and identity lies originates in the work of Dr. Ed Smith, who lists eight wounds in the appendix of *Beyond Tolerable Recovery* (Campbellsville, KY: Alathia, 2000), with their corresponding identity beliefs.

10. Pope John Paul II, *Man and Woman He Created Them: A Theology of the Body* (Boston: Pauline Books and Media, 2006), 27:1.

11. See Pope Francis, "28th World Youth Day, Palm Sunday Homily," March 24, 2013, https://www.vatican.va/content/francesco/en/homilies/2013/documents/papa-francesco_20130324_palme.html.

Bob Schuchts is the bestselling author of *Be Healed*, *Be Transformed*, *Be Devoted*, and *Be Restored*. He is the founder of the John Paul II Healing Center in Tallahassee, Florida, and cohost of the *Restore the Glory* podcast with Jake Khym.

After receiving his doctorate in family relations from Florida State University in 1981, Schuchts became a teacher and counselor. While in private practice, he also taught graduate and undergraduate courses at Florida State and Tallahassee Community College. Schuchts later served on faculty at the Theology of the Body Institute and at the Center for Biblical Studies—where he taught courses on healing, sexuality, and marriage—and was a guest instructor for the Augustine Institute. He volunteered in parish ministry for more than thirty years.

He retired as a marriage and family therapist in December 2014.

Schuchts has two daughters and ten grandchildren. His wife, Margie, died in 2017.

jpiihealingcenter.org
www.restoretheglorypodcast.com
Twitter: @JPIIHealing
Facebook: JP2HealingCenter

Fr. John Burns is a popular speaker and the bestselling author of *Adore* and *Lift Up Your Heart*. He is a priest of the Archdiocese of Milwaukee.

More Healing Books from Bob Schuchts

Be Healed
A Guide to Encountering the Powerful Love of Jesus in Your Life

The bestselling book *Be Healed* is based on Bob Schuchts's popular program for spiritual, emotional, and physical healing. Incorporating elements of charismatic spirituality and steeped in scripture and the wisdom of the Church, this book offers hope in the healing power of God through the Holy Spirit and the sacraments.

ALSO AVAILABLE IN SPANISH!

Be Transformed
The Healing Power of the Sacraments

God has given us the perfect solution to transform our lives and grow spiritually in spite of our sinfulness—the sacraments. In *Be Transformed*, Bob Schuchts demonstrates how each of the seven sacraments is a life-changing encounter with Christ.

Be Devoted
Restoring Friendship, Passion, and Communion in Your Marriage

Bob Schuchts delivers sound Catholic teaching, rich storytelling, and practical tools for healing, along with psychological insights and expertise to help couples to create a relationship that is rich in trust, passion, and unity.

Be Restored
Healing Our Sexual Wounds through Jesus' Merciful Love

In *Be Restored,* Bob Schuchts offers you concrete steps for healing your sexual wounds, relying on a combination of clinical expertise, Catholic theology, and personal experience as a survivor to guide you on your journey to wholeness.